6·13·12 Jo Ann Fabrics

HAND APPLIQUÉ

with *Embroidery*

Sandra Leichner

American Quilter's Society

P. O. Box 3290 · Paducah, KY 42002-3290

www.AmericanQuilter.com

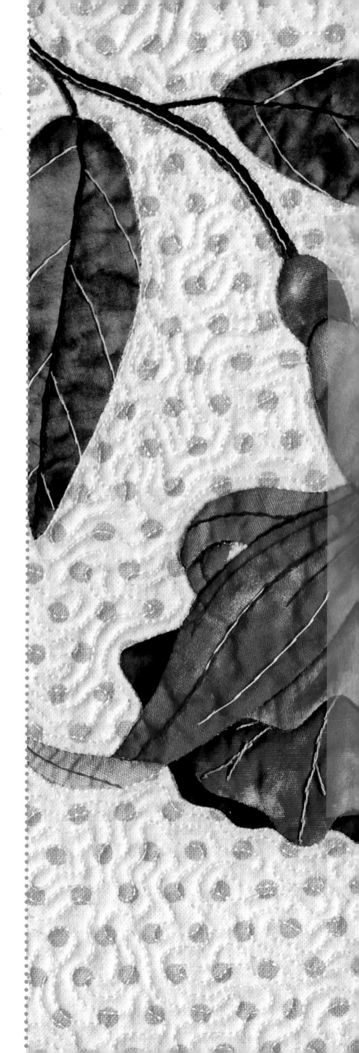

Located in Paducah, Kentucky, the American Quilter's Society (AQS) is dedicated to promoting the accomplishments of today's quilters. Through its publications and events, AQS strives to honor today's quiltmakers and their work and to inspire future creativity and innovation in quiltmaking.

EXECUTIVE BOOK EDITOR: ANDI MILAM REYNOLDS
GRAPHIC DESIGN: ELAINE WILSON
COVER DESIGN: MICHAEL BUCKINGHAM
QUILT PHOTOGRAPHY: CHARLES R. LYNCH, *unless otherwise noted*
HOW-TO PHOTOGRAPHY AND ILLUSTRATIONS: SANDRA LEICHNER

Additional copies of this book may be ordered from the American Quilter's Society, PO Box 3290, Paducah, KY 42002-3290, or online at www.AmericanQuilter.com.

Copyright © 2010, Author, Sandra Leichner
Design © 2010, American Quilter's Society

Library of Congress Cataloging-in-Publication Data

Leichner, Sandra.
  Hand appliqué with embroidery / by Sandra Leichner.
    p. cm.
  ISBN 978-1-57432-677-2
  1. Appliqué--Patterns. 2. Embroidery I. Title.
  TT779.L45 2010
  746.44'5--dc22
                            2010037664

Proudly printed and bound in the United States of America

COVER: TEA WITH MISS D, detail. Full quilt page 70.
TITLE PAGE: LITTLE BIRD, detail. Full quilt page 60.
RIGHT: FUCHSIA, detail. Full quilt page 48.

Dedication

· · · · · · · · · · · · · · · ·

This book is dedicated to
my children—
Andrew, Jason, and Jenna—
and to my husband, Brett.
They have been so supportive
and understanding of my passion
for making quilts.

Contents

· · · · · · · · · · · ·

LEFT: PHARAOH, detail. Full quilt page 93.

Introduction

I have always been intrigued and fascinated by details and the importance of their role as the glue that pulls together all of the visual elements in a design.

My high school art teacher pointed out and impressed upon me just how important those touches of interest can be in making a piece of art—in any medium—successful. Whether your quilts are made for bed use or wall display, it is always the details that make a quilt special and unique. They are the ultimate, personal, creative stamp on a quilt.

Hand appliqué on its own has a limited impact visually, but it is highly adaptable to incorporating embellishments of all kinds. Although each quilter can interpret a pattern differently, in the end the appliqué is left wanting without the details that make it come to life. When a quilt is truly complete, the details the quilter uses set it apart.

Like so many quilters, I grew up with a needle and thread in my hand creating various forms of needlework. It was a natural fit to blend these other needlework skills with appliqué to create unique, beautiful quilts.

With very little extra effort, a basic design can be taken to new levels of visual rewards. None of the embroidery stitches I incorporate into my quilts take great skill or lots of practice. Amazingly, they really don't take a great investment of time, either.

This is the great secret I want to share with other enthusiastic quilters like you—adding details takes not nearly the effort you will get in impact.

This book only begins to cover the multitude of embellishment applications that can be used to accentuate and add texture to your appliqué quilts. I invite you into my world of hand appliqué with embroidery and embellishment to discover your own playground of creativity. It is my desire to encourage you and to help you have more fun and success with your adventures in appliqué. The possibilities truly are endless.

OPPOSITE: TEA WITH MISS D, detail. Full quilt page 70.

Sewing
Needleturn Appliqué

Supplies

Like any other form of art and craft, the tools and materials we choose are very important to what our quiltmaking experiences and end results will be.

The right tools and materials can make all the difference in the ease and quality in which we are able to create our bed quilts, wallhangings, or heirloom quilts. In most cases, you are investing a large amount of time and soul into your quilt, so allow yourself to use the best materials you can afford and you will be rewarded over and over by the end results.

I try almost every new notion that hits the market and continue to experiment when I see something interesting that may make the process more streamlined or help me improve my technique. Admittedly, sometimes the tried, true, and comfortable is hard to improve upon.

With some tools, it may not be a simple case of a one size fits all. My favorite appliqué needle may not work well for you and vice versa. We usually find out fairly quickly what tool is most comfortable for us individually to work with, and we tend to stick with that type and brand. This is okay! Don't deny yourself the right to experiment, however, because you just might discover something that works better for you and makes the process and result much more enjoyable.

Appliqué Needles

The needle is probably one of the most important tools in appliqué.

The right needle can do most of the work for you, from improving stitch quality to correcting the edges of poorly cut pieces as you sew. I have tried various brands and sizes of needles for hand appliqué, but I always return to a #11 sharps. These needles seem to be adaptable to any size

OPPOSITE AND ABOVE: POPPY SOLILOQUY, detail. Full quilt on page 93.

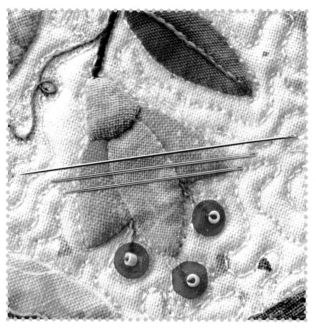

Fig. 1–1. Top: Straw (milliners) needle
Middle: #10 sharps needle
Bottom: #11 sharps needle

Pins

Small pins measuring ½" to ¾" long are best for pin basting appliqué. I prefer pins with small, white, glass, tear-drop shaped heads. The appliqué thread does not catch as easily on the heads of these pins and if the thread does happen to snag, it slides off easily without disturbing my work.

One other major quality I look for in an appliqué pin is the ease with which the pin penetrates and slides through the fabrics. It should be like butter. This is especially important with tightly woven fabrics such as commercial batiks. If you are experiencing resistance when trying to insert a pin into the fabric layers, try another pin (the one you're using may have dulled) or try another type or brand and see if you have better success (Fig. 1–2).

of appliqué piece and are shorter than the usually recommended #10 sharps, giving me more control.

I find straw needles, also known as milliners, too long to achieve nice, small even stitches; they can be difficult to maneuver in tight spaces and on small pieces and circles. Large gentle curves and straight edges may work fine with a straw needle, but if you are a quilter who works with intricately layered appliqué, you may find the straw needle frustrating (Fig. 1–1).

Buy a few sizes of needles in different brands and test them to find out which one works the best for you and achieves the stitch you are comfortable and satisfied with.

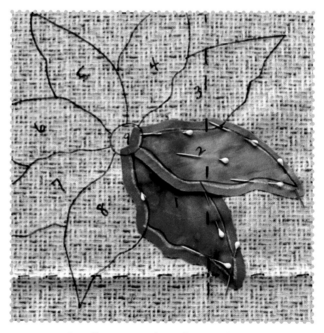

Fig. 1–2. Small pins are best for pin basting appliqué.

Why is this important? With intricate appliqué, it is very important that you do not shift the pieces out of place while pinning. If the tip and shaft of the pin do not slide easily into the layers of fabric, you will get a slight shift in your appliqué placement that will eventually cause major alignment problems down the road.

Freezer Paper

There are many methods and materials on the market for creating templates for appliqué, but I still haven't found a match for freezer paper. If you work with large shapes, template plastic should work fine, but if you do intricately layered appliqué, you will avoid many pitfalls and frustrations if you use a freezer-paper template for needleturn appliqué. Freezer paper is found in your supermarket, usually on the bottom shelf where plastic wrap, wax paper, and aluminum foil are found. You get a lot for a small price.

Sandpaper Board

A sandpaper board has to be one of the best gadgets invented for appliqué. You can avoid line distortion or bias stretch when marking your fabrics around templates that are placed on a piece of sandpaper affixed to a piece of cardboard. This tool makes a huge difference in accuracy. The cleaner the marking line, the more precise the finished edges will be. The sandpaper board makes it effortless to get clean turning lines when marking around templates. Also, bias stretch caused by the pull of the marking tool becomes a non-issue.

Marking Tools

I have definite preferences when it comes to marking tools for appliqué developed after solving many, many problems. I always mark my freezer-paper templates with a number two pencil—not a black permanent pen.

Why is this important? If you use Fray Check™ Sealant to stop frayed threads on inward curves, a black pen's ink used to mark the freezer-paper template will melt on contact with it and travel onto the fabric, staining it. Black ink also creates a thicker marking line than a pencil. If you are working with many small pieces, even a "smidge" of difference in the cutting line can have an impact in how the pieces fit together later. The thinner the marking line, the easier the matching-up process will be as your appliqué reaches completion.

There are so many fabric marking pencil options on the market it can be very confusing as to which one will offer the best results. Experiment to find the one that works best for you. I use a white, non-waxed pencil and have had excellent results. I am loyal to Pat Campbell's or Roxanne's™ white marking pencil.

I do not use a Pigma® permanent pen or pencil to mark around my freezer-paper templates on my fabric. A permanent ink pen or pencil offers no fudge room if the appliqué becomes slightly off and we all need the freedom to adjust those lines once in awhile; those marks are permanent.

Why is this important? A white chalk pencil is easily brushed away. This allows some extra room to fudge the placement and/or seam allowance if the appliqué pieces don't fit perfectly when lining up with the pattern and the other previously appliquéd pieces. There are many washable marker choices available in the marketplace.

Upholstery Vinyl

My favorite method for transferring appliqué patterns, and the most flexible, is using upholstery vinyl as an overlay. I can accurately transfer my designs, even a large quilting pattern, to this plastic. It can be found in most large fabric stores and stores that specialize in upholstery fabrics.

The ease with which you can work with this stuff is amazing. There are several thickness options (measured in millimeters [mm]); I like the 12mm thickness. It is slightly heavier than the 10mm and isn't prone to stretching. (That can cause a whole other set of problems.)

For a light background fabric, trace the pattern lines onto the plastic with a black Sharpie® Ultra Fine permanent pen. For a dark background, transfer the pattern lines with a white or a Pentel® paint pen found in any craft or art supply store. This is the only white pen I have found that will not smear when you apply it to the upholstery vinyl (Fig. 1–3).

Fig. 1–3

Light Table

I use a light table mainly for tracing master patterns from my design illustrations. If the background fabric is light, the light table can be useful for accurately tracing and placing the embroidery lines from the master pattern to the background material. However, when it comes to transferring the appliqué pattern to the fabric, the light table creates more work than is necessary in comparison with the vinyl overlay technique.

Why is this important? Light tables are only so large, and at the most, unless you can afford professional light tables, only allow for a 12" x 12" area to be traced at a time. If you are working with a pattern that has more than a 12" x 12" square area, you will end up with matching and consistency problems. It is not preferable to directly trace to the background fabric because the tracing lines are hard to eliminate later if you choose not to wash the finished quilt.

Another problem with using a light table is that tracing can become slightly distorted on the fabric due to imperceptible bias stretch from the marking pencil drag. The use of a light table also limits the fabrics you can choose as the background material. Any fabric that has a bold pattern or is medium to dark in color is going to end up being eliminated as a possible choice for a background fabric because the bolder patterns and darker colorations of the fabrics do not allow you to see the tracing lines. Black or near black backgrounds are definitely out as an option with a light table transfer method. I don't like to be limited in my background fabric choices, so I use upholstery vinyl.

Threads

I think I have tried just about every thread on the market to find what behaves and blends the best when it comes to appliqué. Thread is an area of individual preference and opinion. Threads do behave differently and can be a determining factor in how well your stitch is executed. If the thread is too thick, you will have unsightly stitches regardless of how good your stitch technique is. With thread too thin, I find blisters are almost an unavoidable nuisance. (Blisters are those little bumps that occur along the edges of the appliqué when the tension on the thread is off, or fiber weights are mismatched, causing an irregular puckered edge.) I stick to 100% cotton 50 weight 2 ply and 60 weight threads.

Fray Check and Toothpicks

When I was first learning to appliqué I was told these tools were crutches and no self-respecting appliquér would be caught dead with these in their sewing box. But you know what? They helped me do a lot of the hard stuff such as inward points and skinny inward curves without ruining my all of my hard work. My philosophy is, "If it helps then use it!"

Fray Check controls the fray (whiskers) that are almost an automatic nuisance with inward points and curves. A small dot of it on the fabric along the turn line of the inward point or along a skinny inward curve *before* marking around your template, and those little wisps of threads will be under control. This will give you some added insurance to make a controlled, clean turn.

The toothpick is handy in the process of assisting you in turning under the seam allowance in tight situations. The fabric grabs the wood texture of the toothpick and holds on for the turn. The only drawback is that in most cases, the toothpick tends to inadvertently transform an inward point into an inward curve due to its width in comparison to a needle. Just pay careful attention and use the very tip of the toothpick and you should be able to control the distortion.

Thanks to these early training wheels, I am now able to create nice work using just my needle. However, I still keep my old friends around for little appliqué emergencies. Whiskers do not discriminate based on skill level.

Scissors

I love scissors and collect all the kinds that are in abundance on the market today.

Higher quality 3½" to 4" embroidery scissors are excellent for appliqué and embroidery alike. They have precise points and they cut crisply and cleanly straight to the scissor tip, which is very important for accurate inward clipping and trimming (Fig. 1–4).

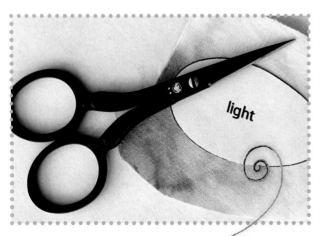

Fig. 1–4

It is also beneficial to have a pair of these sharp, small scissors for cutting templates from freezer paper. Accuracy is really important when cutting out the templates and I don't mind spending a little extra money on a good pair of precision scissors for this purpose. I have been using the same pair for six years now on freezer paper and they are still sharp and precise.

Iron

Any iron that has a cotton setting and a no-steam setting will work fine for ironing the freezer-paper templates to the fabric. Just be careful the iron doesn't get too hot and brown your freezer-paper templates. My iron's setting is usually between medium and high.

Needleturn Technique Tips

The needleturn appliqué method is a very forgiving appliqué technique. It is adaptable to each quilter's individuality, just like a signature.

Needleturn allows for correction at any time during the process of stitching the appliqué to the background material. I sometimes refer to my method of appliqué as the "mutt method." I have combined basic needleturn technique with tricks learned through experience to create a process that works very well for me. As long as the end result is individually satisfactory, I don't think it is of paramount importance what combination of methods and tricks a quilter uses to create appliqué.

Fabric Considerations

The fabrics that are chosen for creating the appliqué have a *huge* impact on how successful the process is going to be for you. The thread count in fabrics is of primary importance because appliqué has to take into account how much of a fray factor the fabric contains.

Loosely woven fabrics held together with large amounts of starch will lead to major frustration and disappointment. The basic test for filtering out unsuitable fabrics, after the feel test, is to hold the fabric up to the light.

If the details in the room are clearly visible through the fabric, put it back on the shelf. Only if the fabric is so unique and appears to be the only choice should an exception be made to try and work with it. This choice should not be made often and be careful to cut a generous seam allowance around the freezer-paper template and trim away the excess as you stitch. This is also a good tip to use if you are using silk as an appliqué material. I use garment interfacing in special circumstances when I want to line sheer and lightweight specialty fabrics such as silk or cotton lawn. Not only does the interfacing stabilize the fabric, but it also eliminates shadowing behind the appliqué by transforming these fabrics from sheer to opaque.

I cut the interfacing to the size of the finished shape of the appliqué. If I were to cut the interfacing to match the cut shape of the appliqué,

I would add too much bulk in the seam allowance, making it difficult to needleturn successfully and visually clunky.

Why is this important? The combination of the feel test and the light test is a quick and simple way to alert you to fabrics with a low thread count or heavily starched, poor quality that will fray.

I rarely cut my pieces on the fabric grain due to the fray factor and in favor of fussy cutting for value and pattern. Problems can be avoided with the fabric fraying (whiskering) if the templates are placed on the bias rather than on the grain of the fabric.

Fraying occurs on an edge that is cut on the grain, whereas minimal fray results when the edge is cut on the bias. In addition, bias-cut edges turn under more smoothly and behave better.

The only time an exception is made to cutting template edges on the bias is when fussy-cutting for a specific pattern or weave. Then it is impossible to eliminate all fraying. Also, there are times when an appliqué piece will inevitably have edges that lie on the grain. However, this problem can be reduced by a great percentage by paying attention to how the templates are placed on the fabric to reduce the number of grain line edges. Cut your pieces on the bias; the results will be great (Figs. 1–5 and 1–6).

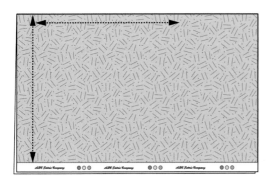

Fig. 1–5

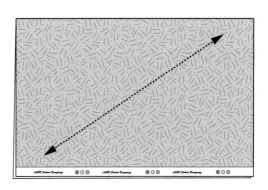

Fig. 1–6

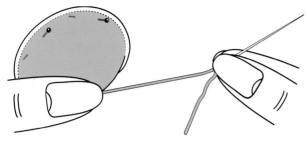

Fig. 1-7

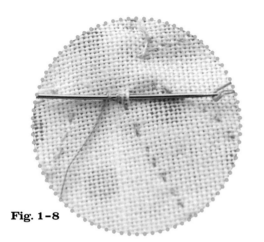

Fig. 1-8

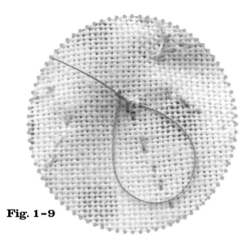

Fig. 1-9

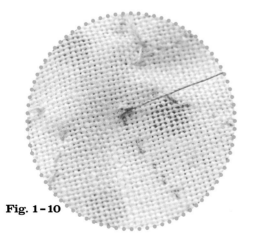

Fig. 1-10

The Appliqué Stitch

I prefer the invisible slipstitch for needleturn appliqué. The needle slides slightly under the appliqué piece and into the background fabric, coming up and catching just the outside edge of the appliqué piece. (Some call this the "bite.")

Holding the edge of the appliqué firmly, but not too tightly, give the thread a slight tug to bury the stitch and it will slightly roll the edge over (Fig. 1–7).

If you do pull the thread too tight and slight puckering occurs, take your finger and gently smooth out the puckers towards the unsewn portion of the appliqué piece. To start the next stitch, insert the needle under the appliqué edge and into the background fabric just behind or into the exit hole of the previous stitch. Bring the needle back up just under the appliqué fold and catch the edge ⅟₁₆" to ⅛" ahead of the last stitch; gently tug to settle the stitch into place. Continue stitching in the same manner.

To secure the thread at the end of stitching, insert the thread and needle slightly under the folded edge of the appliqué and then directly to the back of the work. Next, take the needle and pick up a couple of threads from the background fabric under the appliqué (Fig. 1–8).

Wrap the thread around the needle's shaft twice in the same way you would to make a French knot (Fig. 1–9) and gently pull up the thread while placing your finger gently over the wraps against the fabric (not too tight!). Pull the thread through being careful that it doesn't show on the front of the work (Fig. 1–10). Trim the thread as close to the knot as you want; it will not come loose.

Hand Appliqué with Embroidery ❖ Sandra Leichner

Why is this important? The reason you take a couple of threads of the background fabric is because this prevents the thread tail, however small, from migrating to an area that is visible through the top of the quilt. In essence, you are "parking" the thread tail and it is going nowhere where it can cause havoc in the future. Also, this type of knot-off is almost impossible to undo without snipping into the knot itself.

Watch Out for the Bite

Now then, let's talk some more about that "bite" that is referred to so often when describing the appliqué stitch. In fact, I don't really like that word as a description because it creates a visual suggestion that is often misinterpreted by quilters. The "bite" that is taken by the needle into the appliqué fabric should only be minimal and contain approximately two to three threads of the edge of the appliqué piece. These two threads should be at the very outside edge of the fold of the turned under appliqué seam (Figs. 1–11 and 1–12).

There are many times I have seen appliqué quilts where the stitch bite visibly intrudes into the finished surface of the appliqué piece 1/16" to 1/8". You do not want to see the stitch on the surface of the completed appliqué. An easy way to practice making your stitch invisible, on both the surface and the background, is to use mismatched thread on a practice piece to see where exactly you need to take the "bite" of the appliqué and still create an invisible stitch.

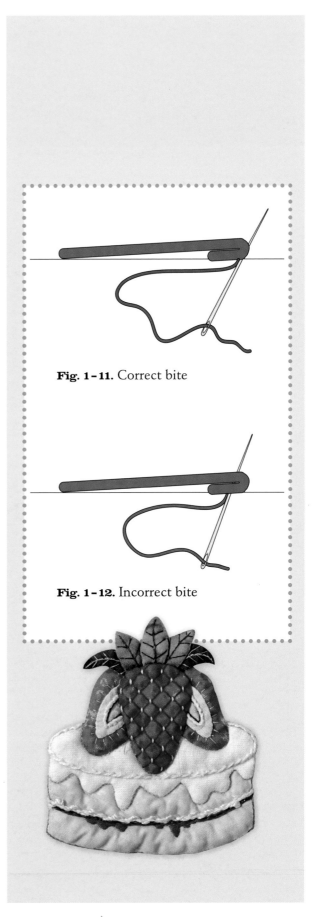

Fig. 1–11. Correct bite

Fig. 1–12. Incorrect bite

What About Seam Allowance?

Seam allowance has a great deal to do with how easily a shape and folded edge is manipulated. Too much seam allowance and you will have great difficulty easing all of that excess fabric underneath the fold. Too little seam allowance and it will wither or fray away and you will have to recut another piece. The optimal seam allowance for needleturn appliqué is a *scant* ³⁄₁₆".

If you are new to handwork and haven't developed sufficient finger dexterity for fine needlework, start with a *generous* ³⁄₁₆" to ¼" seam allowance and either trim as you go or work with larger pieces until you build up skill.

Why is this important? A larger seam allowance creates bulk behind the finished appliqué piece. The smaller the seam allowance, the smoother the finished appliqué will be.

Stitch Length Matters

Stitch length is extremely important to successfully create smooth edges (as opposed to those awkward blisters and bumps that take the pleasure out of appliqué).

A good target to shoot for is a consistent ¹⁄₁₆" stitch length. However, there are times when a larger or smaller stitch can be used or is preferred. The closer your stitches on the curves, the smoother and cleaner the edges will be. Too much space between each stitch results in uneven, rough curves, robbing you of a perfectly rounded edge.

Point Pointers

Points are not scary if you understand how they work and where problems arise. Bulky or rounded points are the result of too much fabric stuffed defiantly into a too small space. This is especially true of tall, skinny points. The right amount of seam allowance is key to creating perfect needleturn appliqué points.

Why is this important? Do not make the mistake of trimming the tip and upper part of the opposite side's seam allowance before creating the point. These are not the areas that are responsible for the added bulk and the difficulty in creating the point. You are actually cutting away necessary seam allowance that is crucial to creating a clean point. All you will have left is a few whiskers of fabric, if you are lucky, to try and turn under.

As you stitch towards the point, reduce the size of your stitches as you reach the pivot. Park your needle to the side (Fig. 1–13). Remove as many pins as necessary to have access to the seam allowance on the unsewn stitched side.

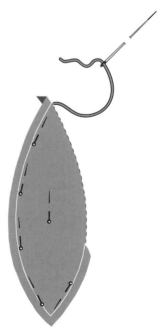

Fig. 1 – 13

Trim away the sewn seam allowance close to the seam up to a scant 1/16" from the pivot point. You should have what I refer to as "the flag" at the tip of the piece (Fig. 1–14).

Repin the appliqué as necessary. Grab the seam allowance and the flag with the point of the needle and sweep it underneath the piece toward the just-sewn side in one smooth move. This should be a much easier task because you now have no seam allowance to work against you from the previous seam (Fig. 1–15).

Tug gently on the thread in a perpendicular motion to the tip of the point and gently pull the tip outward to create a sharper point (Fig. 1–16). Take your needle and coax any wayward fabric back under the fold.

Take the needle directly and completely through to the back of the work at the very tip of the point. Give the thread another gentle tug. Come back up through the background slightly under the appliqué on the opposite side yet to be stitched and then grab a couple of threads with the needle of the appliqué edge (Fig. 1–17).

Take another stitch and you should have a nice pointed tip with no additional bulk. Continue stitching down the other side of the appliqué.

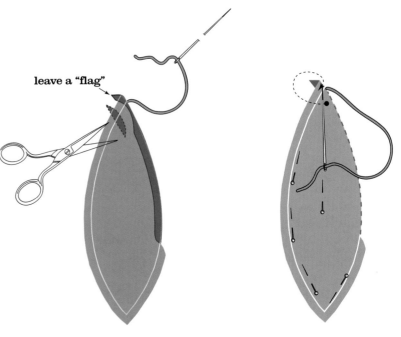

Fig. 1–14   **Fig. 1–15**

leave a "flag"

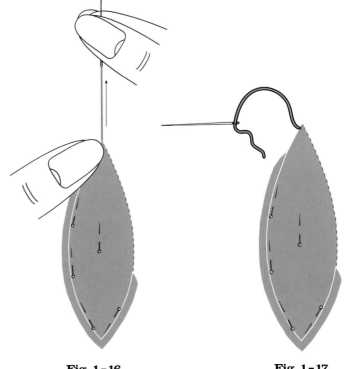

Fig. 1–16   **Fig. 1–17**

Caution on Curves

Curves are easily conquered with just a little extra care. Remember, successful appliqué does not happen with a uniform, consistent stitch-to-the-inch philosophy. Varying the stitch length is important to creating a smooth needleturn curve.

The tighter the curve, the closer together the stitches need to be in relation to each other as the curve steepens. By adjusting stitch length, most of the work will be done for you by the stitching and smooth curves will almost be automatic.

When the curve runs along the straight of grain it becomes difficult to create a smooth and consistent curving edge. If this happens, take your needle and without piercing the fabric, slide it gently back and forth against the underside of the turned seam allowance until it lies properly in place. By "tickling" the turned under seam allowance (belly) this way before stitching, you are able to coax the edge to turn smoothly into shape and avoid creating awkward pleats in your curves that detract visually from the finished appliqué.

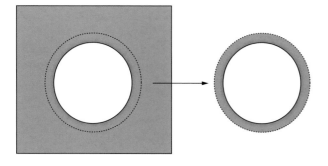

Fig. 1–18

Avoiding Square Circles

Circles seem to give many an appliquér a great deal of grief and cause a groan or two. There are several methods to help achieve nice circular circles. This is my preferred method for tackling those pesky circles large or tiny:

With a pencil trace the circle onto the dull side of freezer paper. Cut out this freezer-paper template and iron it onto the wrong side of the fabric. Cut around the template on the fabric including the scant ³⁄₁₆" seam allowance (Fig. 1–18). (There are new circle template products now on the market that can be helpful.)

Hand Appliqué with Embroidery ❁ Sandra Leichner

Turn the edges over the template and baste down, easing in excess fabric as needed. Manipulate and finger press around the outside edge as needed to eliminate any seam allowance pleats that remain visible. Iron the prepared circle flat (Fig. 1–19).

Fig. 1–19

The next step is to sew the circle onto the background fabric. The key to creating circles that are indeed circular is to take consistent, small, close stitches around the outside edge of the circle. This is also helpful in eliminating little pleats that can appear from easing in the excess seam allowance. Stop a ¼" from the starting point of your stitching, remove the basting stitches, and release the freezer-paper template and remove it. With a toothpick or your needle, turn under the seam allowance of the remaining unsewn edge and stitch it closed (Fig. 1–20).

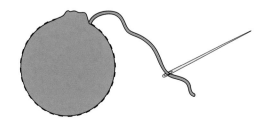

Fig. 1–20

Problem solver: If you feel your circle still has some awkward areas that need attention, stitch around the circle's edge one more time and this should eliminate any remaining problem area(s).

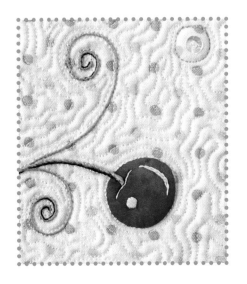

Passing the Starting Line

I have one more tip that can make a big difference in the final appearance of your appliqué. When stitching has been completed around an appliqué piece, if you continue to stitch past your original starting point, the stop and start will blend in seamlessly to the rest of the stitching. No visible sign of beginning or end will be detected.

Embellishing Apéliqué

Appliqué

Nothing adds more interest to an appliqué design than hand embroidery embellishment.

Regardless of whether I incorporate basic or complex stitches, I always experience beautiful results that accentuate and add texture and dimension to my appliqué quilts. Hand embroidery used with appliqué is really not all that time-intensive because it is mainly added in small amounts that take a relatively short amount of time to create.

The idea to keep in mind is that embellishment is just a tool to help compliment the appliqué. It is not intended to share the spotlight or unintentionally become the focal point of the quilt's design.

I have seen too many quilts that exercised the philosophy that if a little is good, more must be

better! This approach sets up the quilt design for failure; the end result tends to be a very busy design that is confusing to look at and has the characteristics of a "painted lady." All of the previous appliqué work has been rendered ineffective and the quilt falls apart visually.

Think of your appliqué like a painting. The appliqué is the overall general work that is the bones and focal point of the main design. This becomes a base that will be further enhanced by the detail work of the embellishment. The embroidery acts as fine brushwork, which has the chief responsibility to marry colors, add texture and detail, or enhance the basic images to give further depth to the appliqué.

Embroidery also can be used to add small images and motifs that can't be successfully appliquéd due to their tiny scale. The photos in Figs. 2–1a and b and 2–2a and b, page 24, illustrate how effective adding a few embroidery details can be.

OPPOSITE AND ABOVE: AMERICAN STILL LIFE, detail. Full quilt page 93.

Fig. 2–1a. Before

Fig. 2–1b. After

Fig. 2–2a. Before

Fig. 2–2b. After

Embroidery Embellishment Materials

Embroidery and Embellishing Needles

The main thing to remember about embroidery needles is to make sure the eye is large enough to accommodate the thread(s) you are using. If the eye of the needle is too small for the thread, the thread will shred, or at the very least, the fibers will be severely weakened.

One other consideration that is somewhat unique to quiltmaking is to take into consideration the size of the needle's shaft compared to the fabric. You want a needle that accommodates the thickness of the thread but won't leave a large hole in the fabric after passing through. If you find the needle is leaving a conspicuous hole after making a stitch, try a smaller size needle and see if that eliminates the problem.

Basic embroidery needles have one of two types of points at the end of their shaft: a sharp penetrating point or a rounded point that does not penetrate the fabric. Each type of needle is intended for a specific use. The following table is a general guide for embroidery needle use. I have had equal success with all brands of needles on the market.

Embroidery and Embellishing Needles		
Needle	**Size**	**Thread Guide**
Sharps *(sewing)* The general purpose needle	10–12	100–30 wt. sewing thread
		1–2 strands of 6-ply cotton embroidery thread
		1–2 strands of silk twist or stranded silk
		1–2 strands MonoPoly™ thread for beading
		1 strand 40 wt. metallic thread
		1 + strands of Kreinik metallic filament
Crewel *(embroidery)*	9–10 3–8	1–3 + strands of 6-ply cotton embroidery thread
		1–2 + stands of silk twist or stranded silk
		1–2 strands of #12 silk twist
		1 strand of #3 & #5 silk Pearl
Chenille *(large eye)*	18–24	silk chenille
		#3 silk Pearl
		Yarns
Tapestry *(blunt tip)*	26–28 18–24	Used for techniques that the needle won't penetrate the threads of the surface fabric and can be used with any of the threads listed above
Straw *(milliners)*	9–11 5–8 1–4	Used primarily for bullion, cast on, and drizzle stitches

Threads

When it comes to embroidery, any thread is fair game as far as I am concerned. There are so many threads available to us today in all kinds of colors, textures, and fibers. My favorite and most prized threads are the silks. I love the silk threads because of their unique luster and the beautiful way they reflect light from the surface of the appliqué. Today you can get silk thread in a variety of twists and weights such as pearl, silk twist, and stranded silk. The list goes on and on and is updated constantly. Just make sure to test for colorfastness if you intend on ever getting your quilt wet.

Cottons are still the workhorses in embroidery, and companies are continually coming up with new colors to match today's fabric color schemes. There are also small cottage companies who are creating cotton threads that are particularly luxurious in a multitude of hand-dyed colors and various weights that give beautiful surface detail. Cotton threads can be found everywhere in various weights, plies, and colors. And don't forget: machine sewing thread can also play double duty for very fine detail embroidery as well.

Specialty threads abound and are so much fun to incorporate into quilts for a touch of whimsy or elegance. If the thread can be threaded through a needle or couched to the surface, it can be used on a quilt. Have fun and experiment and you will be surprised at the variety of options and the inspired results!

Embroidery Hoop

To stabilize an area on the quilt top for embroidery and other embellishment work, there are two preferable sizes of round hoops—4" and 7". The smaller hoop allows you to do more intricate embroidery work with increased flexibility. The larger hoop allows for a larger area to be worked for basic stitching.

Beads

Beads can be very effective when used as an embroidery embellishment on a quilt. There are so many colors and sizes available to us that they can become as addictive as fabric! When used judiciously, beads add sparkle and fun to the quilt's surface. I have found that only Superior Thread's MonoPoly™ thread works to secure the beads to the surface invisibly. It doesn't stretch, which is essential for snug beading that doesn't loosen its tension later. As a bonus, it is heat resistant, which matters when pressing.

Sequins

Sequins alone or combined with beads can add a touch of sparkle to the surface of your quilt and an extra touch of texture, too. Sequins come in many sizes and colors that are great for various effects. My particular favorite is the mini 2mm size. These come in a variety of colors, are so much fun to work with, and give a delicate touch of texture, sparkle, and color.

Thread Considerations

Many of us have experience with some form of needlework using six-ply cotton embroidery threads. These threads are still the workhorse of basic embellishment for appliqué and are great threads to continue working with.

Most of the time, however, even only one strand of a six-ply cotton embroidery thread is too thick and gives a heavy-handed appearance for fine detail. Depending on the piece size that is appliquéd, the appropriate thread weight can vary from a fine sewing thread to several plies of a thicker weight thread.

Because appliqué incorporates many scale changes within the design, a one-size-fits-all thread practice can lead to unfortunate and awkward visual results. You should have a variety of thread weights available to you for embroidery embellishment, from size 100 silk to really thick yarns.

For example, facial features are usually more believable when a 50- or 40-weight sewing thread is used to embroider the features of the face.

That said, the new yarns being created for knitters are fantastic for adding texture to appliqué. Uses include creating a dimensional, realistic bird nest or mossy texture on trees and stones.

Why is this important? I can't stress this point enough: you must consider the scale of the appliqué piece when considering the appropriate weight of threads for adding detail.

Be sure to test for colorfastness with any specialty thread to avoid any disasters down the road when wet blocking or washing your finished quilt. I soak a sample of the threads in water and then place them on top of a white piece of fabric to air dry. If there is any dye that will bleed, it will be wicked by the white fabric as it dries and you will know if it is a "don't use" thread.

Embroidery Stitches

The patterns in this book use basic embroidery stitches. Follow my lead to understand how simple stitches, looked at differently, can take your appliqué to a higher level of interest and beauty.

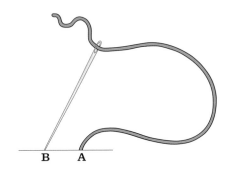

Fig. 2–3

Straight Stitch and Satin Stitch

Straight stitches can be used to suggest details, add touches of color, or be employed to create images that are too small and intricate to apply with appliqué. The straight stitch and the satin stitch are an important part of the toolbox for accentuating appliqué (Figs. 2–3 and 2–4).

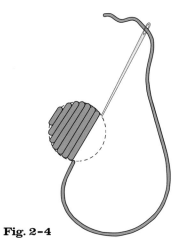

Fig. 2–4

The straight stitch can be used to hint at details such as the feather fluff on this bird (Fig. 2–5) and the "stems" of the stamens. Are small eyes such as this bird's too small for appliqué comfort? Use the satin stitch to fill the area (Fig. 2–6).

Fig. 2–5   **Fig. 2–6**

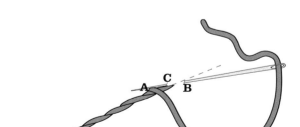

Fig. 2–7. The needle emerges midway to the left of the previous stitch (A), then is inserted into the fabric at (B) about half the distance of the full stitch, then re-emerges just to the left of the exit point of the previously completed stitch (C). Try to make each stitch a consistent length, especially when laying the stitches down as a base for whipping.

Stem/Outline Stitch

Stem stitch and outline stitch are workhorses for adding simple, unobtrusive detail and touches of alternate color. Both stitches are the same in appearance. The difference is whether you make the stitch with the loose thread "up" or "down." I make the stitch with the thread in the down position (Fig. 2–7). Use either stitch to create the veins on leaves or small stems. Either stitch is the base stitch for working the whipped stem stitch (page 32).

Hand Appliqué with Embroidery ❀ Sandra Leichner

The stem/outline stitch is very effective as leaf veins. Try using complementary colors for the veins vs. the leaf color to add more depth and color interest. Veins don't have to be boring! Small, fine stems and drawn details, such as the highlights on the cherry, are perfect for this stitch (Fig. 2–8). The spoon uses a combination of straight stitch and stem stitch for realistic effect (Fig. 2–9).

Fig. 2–8

Fig. 2–9

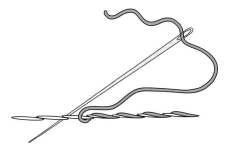

Fig. 2-10. First, work a consistent length stem stitch (outline stitch). To whip, slide the needle under the stitch without catching the fabric using either method A, where two stitches meet (as shown), or method B, underneath a single stitch. I prefer method A because it makes a more solid and tighter line that doesn't budge on the surface than method B.

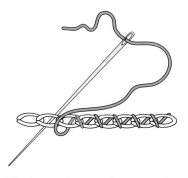

Fig. 2-11. Work consistent chain stitches. To whip, slide the needle under each loop without piercing the fabric wrapping the thread around each chain stitch. The wrapped chain stitch is chunkier than the whipped stem stitch and is useful for larger (thicker) stems.

Fig. 2-12

Whipped Stem and Chain Stitches

A whipped stitch (stem or chain) is easy and essential to create an elegant, finished appearance to details such as tendrils, stems, and whimsical touches that are meant to catch the eye (Fig. 2–12). Compared to a plain stem or chain stitch, a whipped stitch is more solid in texture and appearance.

Amazingly realistic tendrils can be accomplished with the whipped stem stitch (Fig. 2–13). Adjust your thread weight and strand numbers for different scales and sizes of tendrils:

* Thick tendrils: use two strands of DMC® embroidery floss or silk floss
* Delicate tendrils: use one strand of DMC floss or silk floss
* Superfine tendrils: use one strand of 50-wt. or 40-wt. sewing thread

Fig. 2-13

Hand Appliqué with Embroidery ❋ Sandra Leichner

For tightly wound small tendrils like these in the grape illustration (Fig. 2–14), reduce the size of your stem stitches to quite small in length. These tendrils may look difficult at first glance, but are just as simple as the large ones—they just require smaller stitches and more of them.

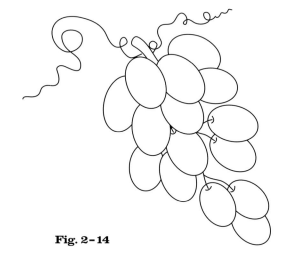

Fig. 2–14

Backstitch

This stitch is particularly useful for outlining images and text (Fig. 2–15). It hugs nicely to the stitching line to create a consistent, uniform line with no tension pull (Fig. 2–16).

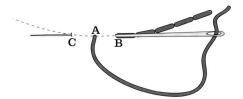

Fig. 2–15

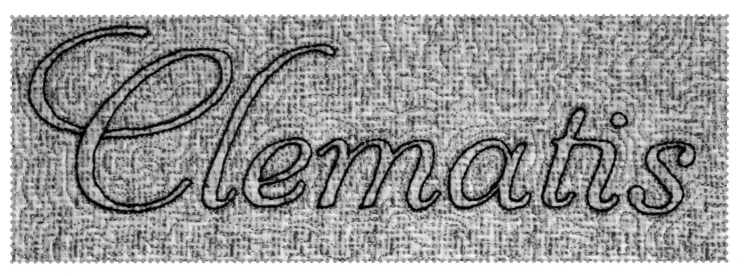

Fig. 2–16

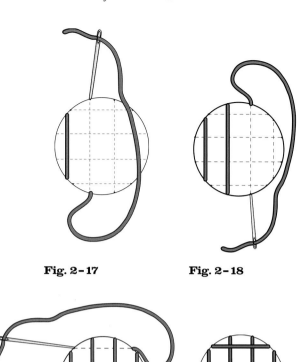

Fig. 2–17   **Fig. 2–18**

Fig. 2–19   **Fig. 2–20**

Fig. 2–21   **Fig. 2–22**

Lattice Couching

Lattice couching is a fill technique that creates texture, depth, and textural interest. A series of crosshatched straight stitches are laid down and then couched down with small stitches to secure the stitch intersections. Lattice couching is very effective for whimsical and decorative fills for an additional visual punch (Figs. 2–17 thru 2–22).

Just by adding simple lattice couching to these center circles (Fig. 2–23) and strawberry (Fig. 2–24), the appliqué is instantly elevated to another level. Try using a darker value for the horizontal stitches and a light value for the vertical stitches. This will give the added illusion of depth.

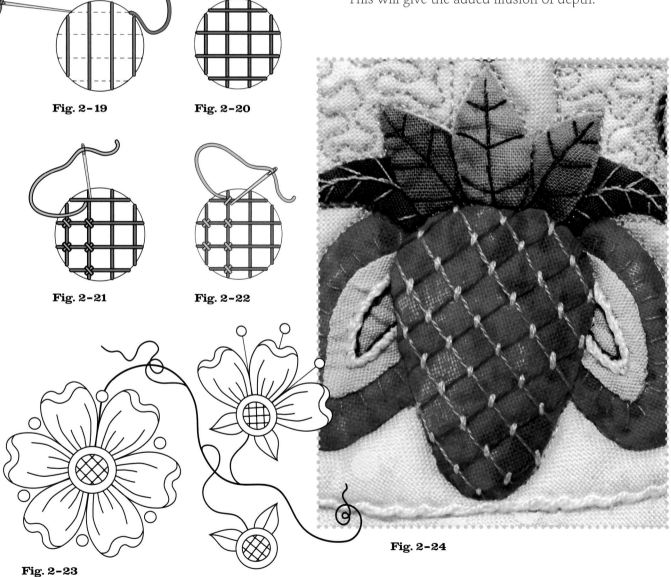

Fig. 2–24

Fig. 2–23

Hand Appliqué with Embroidery ❁ Sandra Leichner

Threaded Running Stitch

I use this as a purely decorative stitch that adds an extra touch of color and design interest. Create the running stitch in one color and thread the running stitch with another to create more depth (Figs. 2–25 and 2–26).

You can see how the bottom of the teabag would be rather plain without this added stitch detail to add design interest and another layer of color (Fig. 2–27). I have staggered my running stitch in this example to create an emphasized wave pattern (Fig. 2–28).

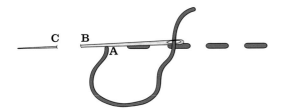

Fig. 2–25

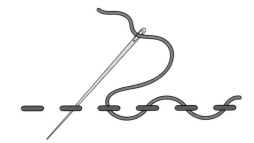

Fig. 2–26

Fig. 2–27

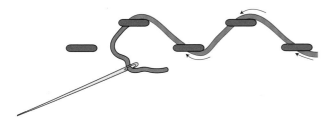

Fig. 2–28

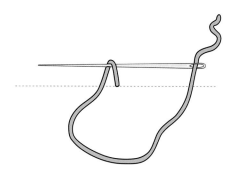

Fig. 2–29a

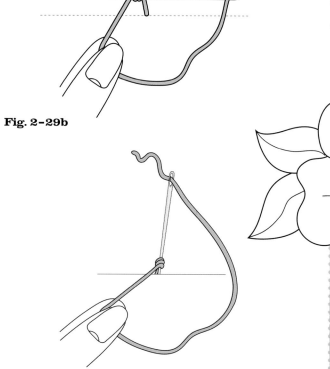

Fig. 2–29b

French Knot

French knots serve a dual purpose. They add instant detail and also great dimension to the appliqué creating texture on the surface. The average French knot is made using two or three wraps. If you would like a bulkier knot, increase the number of threads rather than the wraps to ensure a nice tight knot that holds its shape (Figs. 2–29a–c).

The tips of the stamens on roses are perfect for employing the French knot. Use three different color values individually (light, medium, and dark) to create depth and a more realistic appearance (Fig. 2–30).

Fig. 2–29c. Insert the needle where needle previously exited and with your other hand, hold the thread taut as you pull the thread through to the back for a perfect knot.

Fig. 2–30

Hand Appliqué with Embroidery ❄ Sandra Leichner

Bullion Stitch

Like the French knot, the bullion knot adds dimensional and textural interest to the surface. I love to use these stitches for the tips of stamens. The bullion knot does take a bit of practice to get a feel for the number of wraps needed in relation to the stitch's length. Use a straw needle because its shaft is long and thin, which eliminates most of the difficulty of pulling the needle through without losing control of the wraps (Figs. 2–31 thru 2–36).

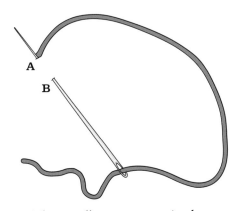

Fig. 2–31. The needle re-emerges in the same hole as "A."

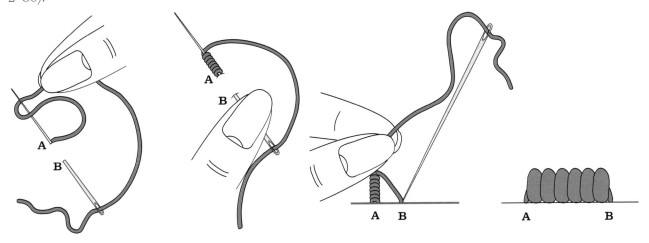

Fig. 2–32   **Fig. 2–33**   **Fig. 2–34**   **Fig. 2–35.** Finished bullion

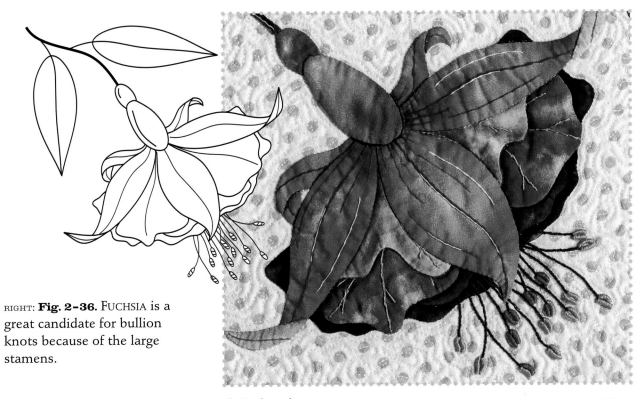

RIGHT: **Fig. 2–36.** FUCHSIA is a great candidate for bullion knots because of the large stamens.

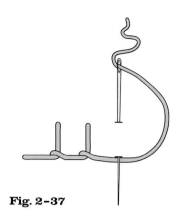

Fig. 2-37

Fig. 2-38

Buttonhole Stitch

The buttonhole stitch is commonly seen as an edge treatment on primitive-style appliqué, but with imagination the buttonhole stitch can be used for creating more elegant decorative embroidered effects and textures (Fig. 2–37).

A lacy painted effect can be accomplished by creating a line of buttonhole stitches as a trim on the teacup for a really nice detail (Figs. 2–38 and 2–39).

The buttonhole wheel is a great decorative stitch and I like to use it for hanging tags where the punch hole is located (Fig. 5-11 on page 68). Vintage embroidery incorporates the buttonhole wheel in a lot of designs so if you are looking to mimic that vintage feel, this is a great stitch with which to do that (Figs. 2–40 through 2–42).

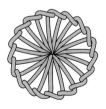

Fig. 2-39

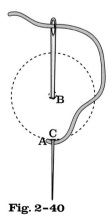

Fig. 2-40

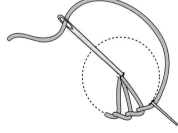
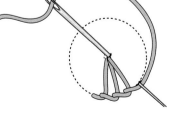

Fig. 2-41

Fig. 2-42

Chain Stitch

The most used and versatile loop stitches for adding detail to appliqué are the chain and the detached chain, also known as the lazy daisy stitch and daisy stitch. The chain stitch can be used to lay a base for a whipped chain stitch to be used for chunkier flower stems. It can also be used as a fill stitch that adds more surface texture (Figs. 2–43a and b). The daisy (detached chain) is effective as an accent stitch or to imply small leaves or petals that are too small to appliqué (Figs. 2–44 and 2–45).

Instead of doing the expected, add a touch of whimsy for leaves and use the chain stitch for an added textural effect (Fig 2–46). Different weights of thread will produce different results so have fun and experiment with scale. An open daisy stitch is also perfect for creating the "thighs" of a bee (Fig. 2–47).

Fig. 2–43a. Chain stitch

Fig. 2–43b. Chain stitch

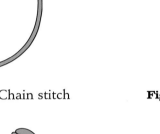

Fig. 2–44. Detached chain stitch

Fig. 2–45. Open chain stitch

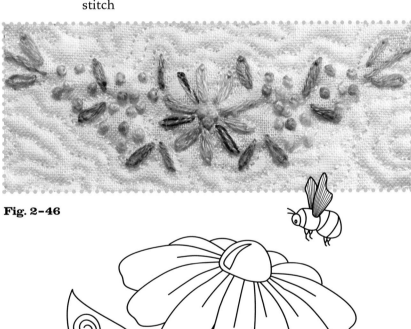

Fig. 2–46

Fig. 2–47

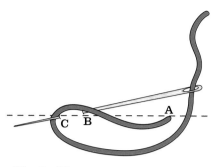

Fig. 2-48

Fig. 2-49

Twisted Chain Stitch

The twisted chain stitch is a great stitch for adding more detailed texture; it is chunkier than the basic chain stitch. It is excellent for giving the illusion of braids and creating raised textured edges (Figs. 2–48 and 2–49).

See how well the twisted chain stitch works for adding a piped edge of whipped cream or frosting to the edge of the strawberry shortcake (Fig. 2–50)? Braids on the Egyptian goddess from PHARAOH were easily created with this stitch (Fig. 2–51). Try combining a metallic or glossy thread with the floss to create a shimmer within the texture.

Fig. 2-50

Fig. 2-51

Hand Appliqué with Embroidery ✷ Sandra Leichner

Turkey Stitch

The Turkey stitch is a dimensional stitch used to add texture to the surface. I use this stitch primarily for adding fuzzy areas to the appliqué such as the center fuzz of a clematis flower or the beard of an iris. Many insects that have fuzzy bodies are good candidates for the Turkey stitch, such as a bee or dragonfly thorax. Use 2–4 strands in the needle. The more threads used, the denser the fill (Figs. 2–52a–d thru 2–54a–b).

The flower centers in CLEMATIS are perfect areas to use the Turkey stitch for a realistic and dimensional effect (Fig. 2–55). Try using two values (light and dark) of thread to create light and shadow automatically.

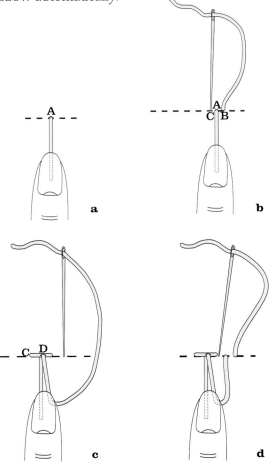

Fig. 2-52a–d. Take the needle to back at (A), pull thread through leaving a tail on the front while holding the thread tail as you are pulling the needle through to the back.

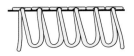

Fig. 2-53. Continue filling area with loops. Do not knot off at the end, but leave a tail just as you did at the beginning.

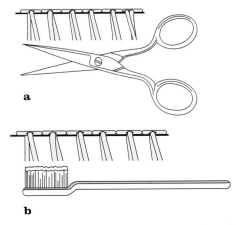

Fig. 2-54a–b. Cut loops to desired length and fluff with a cosmetic brow brush or toothbrush.

BELOW: **Fig. 2-55.** CLEMATIS

Beads and Sequins

Beads and sequins can add incredible sparkle and a touch of additional interest to the surface of appliqué. They are completely washable and can endure some rough treatment. Just be careful to avoid the plastic beads that are found pre-packaged on the craft aisles. I prefer Japanese glass beads because the hole can accommodate a #10 sharps needle easily; they come in hundreds of colors, sizes, and types.

Sequins sometimes have a bad reputation for being less than elegant when used on the surface of a quilt, especially on traditional style quilts. I disagree. Today's sequins come in popular fabric colors and can add additional interest and whimsy to a design. Play and have fun with embellishments on your quilts.

A caution for the uninitiated: dense application of these hypnotic shiny objects on the surface of a predominately appliquéd quilt is usually not a desirable outcome. Trust me on this. As with most embellishing, the details should be discovered upon closer inspection by the viewer.

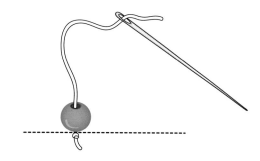

Fig. 2–56

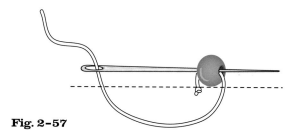

Fig. 2–57

Adding Beads to Appliqué

I have switched to using a clear monofilament polyester thread to attach beads to my appliqué because it is strong enough to secure the beads, but is also invisible and blends with any color(s) of fabric I may use.

Why is this important? Typical beading threads are thick and are obvious to the eye.

To attach a single bead to the surface, use a beading thread with a #10 sharps needle and come up from the back of your work through the center hole of the bead (Fig. 2–56).

Hand Appliqué with Embroidery ❋ Sandra Leichner

To make the bead sit on its side, take the needle to the back close beside the thread. This will make the bead turn on its side. Bring the needle back up through the bead again and then to the back once more; knot off (Fig. 2–57, page 42).

To make the bead lay flat, follow the previous step, except with your hand positioning the bead flat with the hole upward, take a stitch through to the back next to the outside edge of the bead, come back up through the center and back down on the opposite side. Knot off (Figs. 2–58 thru 2–60).

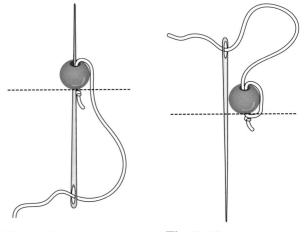

Fig. 2-58   **Fig. 2-59**

Fig. 2-60

Stitching with Sequins

Sequins can add so much fun and whimsy to a quilt's surface. Don't be afraid to play with these sparklers as an embellishment to your appliqué. Unlike the materials our ancestors used, sequins today are not covered with a metallic coating that will eventually flake off. There are so many new sizes and colors on the market that they can become as addictive as beads. Use a light hand and you will be very happy with the results (Figs. 2–61 thru 2–63).

Fig. 2-61

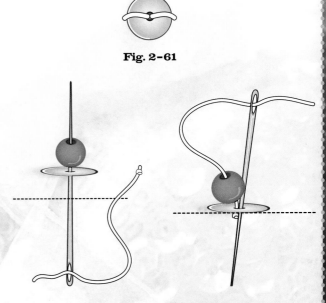

Fig. 2-62   **Fig. 2-63**

General
Preparation Tips

Block Size

I always cut my background pieces for appliqué approximately 2" larger than the finished measurement of the block. By allowing extra fabric in the cut size, you can easily square up the block when it is finished to its correct dimensions. It is far better to have more waste fabric than to end up with a block or border that can't be squared up correctly after all of your invested time and hand work.

Why is this important? Appliqué and especially embroidery tend to shrink and distort the background fabric as you work.

Numbering the Puzzle Pieces

Determining the sequence of construction on a layered appliqué design is a bit like putting a jigsaw puzzle together. The patterns in this book are layered appliqué, which means there can be many pieces that fit on top of each other to form the finished design. These individual pieces are sequentially

OPPOSITE: **UNEXPECTED BEAUTY,** detail. Full quilt on page 93.

numbered to indicate the proper order in which to stitch the pieces onto the background. Feel free to use a different order if it works better for you and your method of working.

Divide and Conquer

With more complex appliqué patterns, break down and isolate areas in a four-square grid and designate them as A, B, C, and D. Because the most underneath pieces are easier to locate this way, stitch order in each section becomes relatively clear. Numbering can be broken down to A1, B1, for example, making the process of following the placement as you appliqué easier.

Mark the Grid

Take time to accurately mark the horizontal and vertical lines of center and the center mark itself on your background fabric with a washable marker. Pay close attention to grain line and you will avoid bias stretch, which will enable you to square up each block or the quilt top easily and have your finished work lay smooth and flat upon completion.

Marking these lines is really important to matching up your work to the pattern and to accurately match up the appliqué pieces with the overlay each time.

Eliminate Excess Fabric

Cut hidden seam allowances the same as you cut the turned-under seam allowances (see page 18). Cutting the hidden seam allowances large and sloppy will show up as shadowing, create unwanted textural bulk, and make visible appliqué fabric lines on the surface. All of this extra fabric will add up piece by piece as you proceed forward with your appliqué. Most of the time there should only be two layers of fabric, plus the background layer, at most, where the seam allowances add up together.

My little bird is always near my side in the garden.

Fabric Notes

I select appliqué fabrics based on their tonal qualities. I usually compile a large selection of fabrics in mainly ½ yard cuts that have at least a two-step value separation between them for a selection of light, medium, and dark gradations that will automatically create shading and depth without much effort on my part.

Why is this important? Because not only do I look for color values in selecting my fabric, but I also fussy cut with my templates for value within the fabric as well. I truly do end up with "Swiss cheese cloth" and some amount of waste of a half yard, but I get exactly the right coloration and values for my appliqué pieces. This is what makes my appliqué stand out.

Solid color fabrics or fabrics with busy prints create a whimsical, folksy, flat appearance rather than a painterly effect as the final outcome. Look for tone-on-tone and small prints that read as a solid and they will respond magically with the embroidery embellishment enhancements you add.

Batiks are wonderful but be careful of the higher thread counts. Other than that little caution, they are magic for bringing life to appliqué and batiks make up a large part of my stash.

Why is this important? A higher thread count is stiff and really difficult to get your needle through. You can feel them instantly because they have the same feel as crisp bed sheets.

LEFT AND OPPOSITE: LITTLE BIRD, detail. Full quilt on page 60.

Projects

. . . .

These projects range in complexity and amount of appliqué and time involved. Those that are relatively easy and can be completed in days I call "instant gratification hand appliqué quilts." The largest project can take much longer and is a bit more challenging.

All fabric requirements are based on 40" wide fabric. A ¼" seam allowance is used unless otherwise noted.

I have not given specific embroidery thread colors because fabric choices will differ and so will brands of threads and availability. Be sure to check out your sewing and appliqué thread collection for some sewing weight thread choices. The cotton floss recommendations are based on the six strand cotton floss commercially available in embroidery shops and craft stores.

Why is this important?
Choosing different values of the thread colors and weights will give your work fantastic depth.

FUCHSIA, 11" x 13¼"

Hand Appliqué with Embroidery ❖ Sandra Leichner

FUCHSIA

I have a very small sewing room and small quilt projects like this Fuchsia design allow me to hang my work to enjoy and yet not overwhelm the walls and limited space. The design can also be made into a nice accent pillow for the home.

Embroidery Stitches

Stem stitch
Whipped stem stitch
Bullion knot

Fabric Requirements

Center appliqué background – 1 fat quarter
Border A – 1 fat quarter
Border B – 1 fat eighth
Appliqué – Assorted fat quarters and scraps

Embellishment Requirements

Suggested Threads

Six-ply cotton embroidery floss
50- or 60-wt. sewing thread

Suggested Needles

#10 sharps for one strand of embroidery floss
    or sewing weight thread
#9 crewel (embroidery) needle for 2–3 strands
    of embroidery floss

Appliqué Pattern

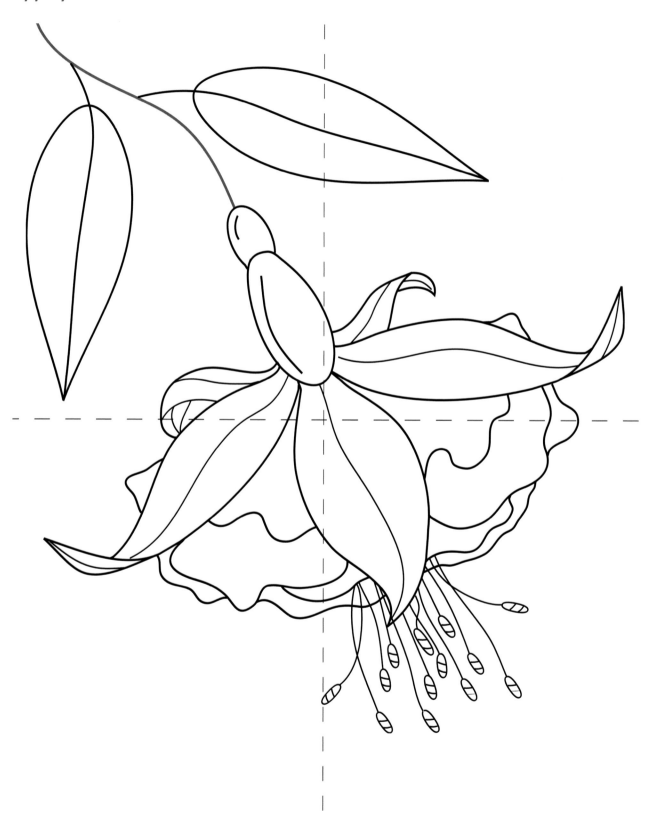

Hand Appliqué with Embroidery ❋ Sandra Leichner

Appliqué Block

For the appliqué background cut a rectangle 9" x 13" (Fig. 3–1).

Embellishment Instructions

Fuchsia Flower (Figs. 3–2 and 3–3)

Add as many or as few veins on the flower sepals as you want. Try adding a really light color to hint at a highlight here and there. When you mark your veins, think of them as roads with forks off to each side, but the roads are staggered.

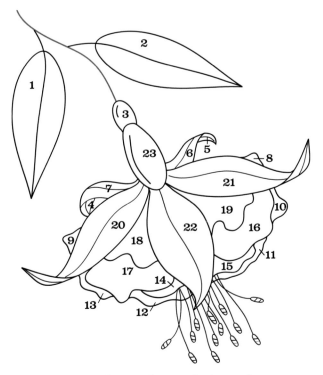

Fig. 3–1. Numbers indicate piecing order.

Fig. 3–2

Fig. 3–3

Fuchsia Flower		
embroidery key #	# strands/thread	stitch
1: upper flower veins	1/cotton floss	stem
2: lower flower veins	1/sewing weight	stem and straight

Leaves and Stem (Figs. 3–4 and 3–5)

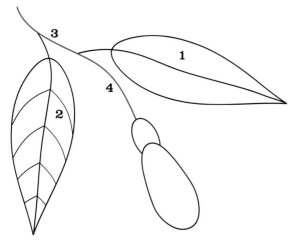

Fig. 3–4

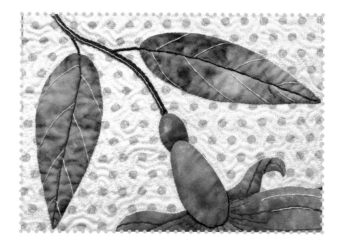

Fig. 3–5

Leaves and Stem		
embroidery key #	**# strands/thread**	**stitch**
1: main vein	1/cotton floss	stem
2: secondary veins	1/sewing weight	stem
3: stem	2/cotton floss	stem (3 rows together)
4: highlight	1/sewing weight	1 stem (on top of stem stitch rows)

Flower Pistils (Figs. 3–6 and 3–7)

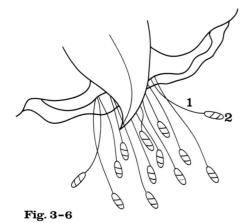

Fig. 3–6

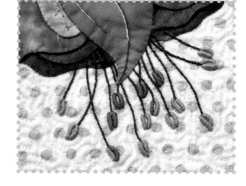

Fig. 3–7

Flower Pistils		
embroidery key #	**# strands/thread**	**stitch**
1: pistil stems	1/cotton floss	whipped stem
2: pistil tips	1/cotton floss	bullion knot

Cutting Instructions

Center: cut appliquéd background to 7½" x 8¾".

Border measurements are for butted borders.

Border A:

Sides: cut 2 strips, 1¾" x 8¾"
Top and Bottom: cut 2 strips, 2¼" x 10"

Border B:

Sides: cut 2 strips, 1" x 11"
Top and bottom: cut 2 strips, 1" x 13¼"

Quilt Assembly

Attach Border A left and right sections to appliqué center (Fig. 3–8).

Attach Border A top and bottom sections to previously sewn section (Fig. 3–9).

Repeat previous steps for Border B (Figs. 3–10 and 3–11).

Square the top, layer, quilt, and bind.

Fig. 3-8

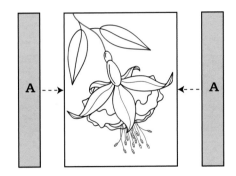

Fig. 3-9

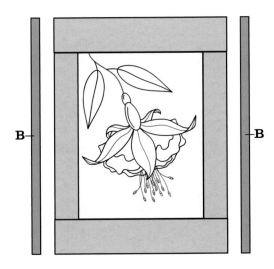

Fig. 3-10

Fig. 3-11

CLEMATIS, 13" x 13"

Hand Appliqué with Embroidery ❖ Sandra Leichner

CLEMATIS

This block would be quite pretty squared up and made into a square pillow, or made into a simple wall quilt by squaring, quilting, and then binding it as is.

Embroidery Stitches

Stem stitch

Whipped stem stitch

Turkey stitch

Fabric Requirements

Center appliqué background – 1 fat quarter

Appliqué – assorted fat quarters and scraps

Embellishment Requirements

Suggested Threads

Six-ply cotton embroidery floss

50- or 60-wt. sewing thread

Suggested Needles

#10 sharps for one strand of embroidery floss or sewing weight thread

#9 crewel (embroidery) needle for 2–3 strands of embroidery floss

Appliqué Pattern

Appliqué Block

For the appliqué background cut a square 14"
x 14". This includes extra "hoop" room for the text
embroidery (Fig. 4–1).

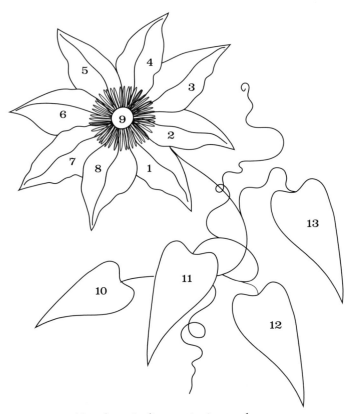

Embellishment Instructions

Leaves, Stems, and Tendrils

(Figs. 4–2 and 4–3)

Fig. 4–1. Numbers indicate piecing order.

Fig. 4–2

Fig. 4–3

Leaves, Stems, and Tendrils		
embroidery key #	**# strands/thread**	**stitch**
1: all stems	2/cotton floss	stem (2 rows side by side)
2: tendrils	2/cotton floss	whipped stem
3: leaf veins	1/cotton floss	stem

Clematis Flower

Add as many or as few veins to the petals as you want. Also try combining three different values or colors of thread for more depth and fun (Figs. 4–4 and 4–5).

Fig. 4–4

Fig. 4–5

Clematis Flower		
embroidery key #	**# strands/thread**	**stitch**
1: flower veins	1/sewing weight	stem
2: center fluff	3/cotton floss	Turkey stitch

Hand Appliqué with Embroidery ❀ Sandra Leichner

Clematis Text (optional)

(Figs. 4–6 and 4–7)

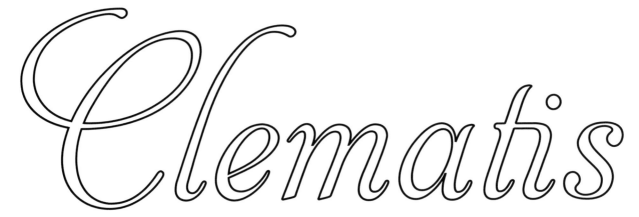

Fig. 4–6. Text template – shown at 100%

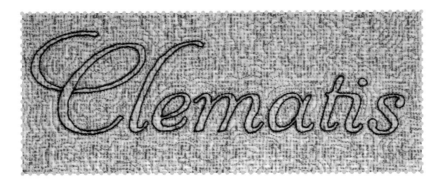

Fig. 4–7

Clematis Text		
embroidery key #	# strands/thread	stitch
1: text outline	2/cotton floss	stem or backstitch

Quilt Assembly

After appliqué and embellishment are complete, square and trim the center block to 13" x 13", then quilt and bind it to make a simple wall quilt.

LITTLE BIRD, 15" x 14"

Hand Appliqué with Embroidery ❉ Sandra Leichner

LITTLE BIRD

Finish this project as a small wall quilt by squaring, quilting, and binding it.

Embroidery Stitches

Stem stitch

Straight stitch

French knot

Satin stitch

Whipped stem stitch

Buttonhole wheel stitch for optional tag

Fabric Requirements

Background fabric for appliqué center –
  1 fat quarter

Border B – 1 fat eighth

Border C – 1 fat eighth

Appliqué – assorted fat quarters and scraps

Embellishment Requirements

Suggested Threads

Six-ply cotton embroidery floss

50- or 60-wt. sewing thread

Suggested Needles

#10 sharps for one strand of embroidery floss
  or sewing weight thread

#9 crewel (embroidery) needle for 2–3 strands
  of embroidery floss

Optional

7mm silk ribbon for border treatment

Appliqué Pattern

Hand Appliqué with Embroidery ❁ Sandra Leichner

Appliqué Pattern

Appliqué Block

For the appliqué background, cut a square 13" x 13" (Fig. 5–1).

Fig. 5–1. Fold under and gently finger press the seam allowance of #14a and pin so it gets caught under the rose petal as the petal is appliquéd down. The main bulk of the leaf (#27) will be left loose and completed later after the bird belly piece (#26) has been appliquéd.

Embellishment Instructions

Bird (Figs. 5–2 and 5–3)

Stitching order: If you choose to appliqué the black center of the bird's eye, skip the satin stitch and start at the straight stitch (2 side-by-side stitches) and continue. Follow the eye instructions in the order written for best results.

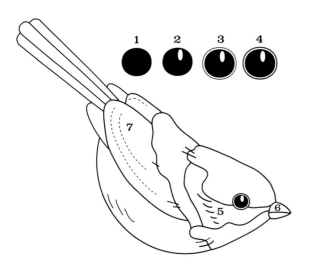

Fig. 5–2

Fig. 5–3

Bird		
embroidery key #	**# strands/thread**	**stitch**
1: center eye	2/cotton floss	satin
2: eye highlight	1/cotton floss	straight (2 side-by-side stitches)
3: white eye surround	1/sewing weight	stem or backstitch
4: golden eye surround	1/sewing weight	stem or backstitch
5: feather fluff	1/cotton floss	straight
6: beak separation	1/sewing weight	stem or backstitch
7: rear feathers	1/sewing weight	stem or backstitch

Rose (Figs. 5–4 and 5–5)

The pistil stitch combines the French knot and straight stitch together in one stitch. However, unless you are using multiple strands, the result is rather wimpy. This is why I prefer to lay straight stitches first, and then go back and do the French knots separately.

Fig. 5–4

Fig. 5–5

Rose		
embroidery key #	**# strands/thread**	**stitch**
1: pistil stems center	1/sewing weight	straight
2: pistil heads	1/cotton floss	French knot (3 wraps)
3: petal veins	1/sewing weight	stem or backstitch

Grapes (Figs. 5–6 and 5–7, page 67)

Grapes		
embroidery key #	**# strands/thread**	**stitch**
1: grape stems	1/cotton floss	whipped stem
2: grape highlight	1/sewing weight	stem or backstitch

Hand Appliqué with Embroidery ❋ Sandra Leichner

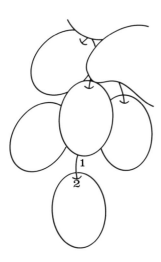

Fig. 5–6

Fig. 5–7

Leaves, Stems, and Tendrils (Figs. 5–8 and 5–9)

Use this key for all leaves, stems, and tendrils in this project.

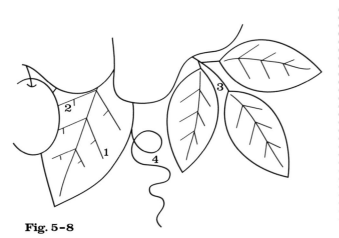

Fig. 5–8

Fig. 5–9

Leaves, Stems, and Tendrils		
embroidery key #	**# strands/thread**	**stitch**
1: main veins all	1/cotton floss	stem
2: large leaves tiny veins	1/cotton floss	straight
3: leaf stems	2/cotton floss	whipped stem
4: tendrils	2/cotton floss	whipped stem

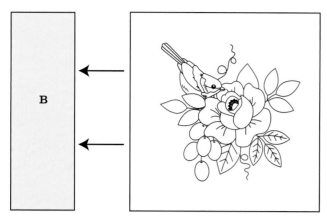

Fig. 5–10

Quilt Assembly

If you plan to apply the optional tag and ribbon embellishment, please read through all of the instructions before you begin.

After appliqué and embellishment are complete, square and trim the center block (A) to 12½" x 12½".

Border measurements are for butted borders.

Border B

Cut (1) strip, 3½" x 12½".

Border C

Cut (2) strips, 1½" x 15½" (Fig. 5–10).

Optional ribbon and tag embellishment

Place the ribbon and tag on the sewn A and B section so that the ribbon will be caught in the seam when attaching border C. The ribbon is tacked to the surface by stitching it down with French knots every half inch along its length (Fig. 5–11).

Mark around the tag template onto chosen fabric, but do not trim the seam allowance at this point (Fig. 5–12, page 69).

Mark the string hole lightly with a washable marking pen. Create the string hole with 2 strands of cotton floss using a buttonhole wheel stitch.

Fig. 5–11

Hand Appliqué with Embroidery ❋ Sandra Leichner

Print your preferred quote and style of text from your computer, scaled to size. Trace it with a fine point fabric pen onto the label and heat set the ink with a hot dry iron. Cut out the label including the seam allowance.

Appliqué the tag to the quilt background (Fig. 5–13). Attach the top and bottom borders (C), square up the top, quilt, and bind (Fig. 5–14).

After quilting and binding is complete, make a separate ribbon bow and place it where the two strips of ribbon cross over each other. Attach it with a few secure hand stitches (See Fig. 5–11, page 68).

Fig. 5-12. Full-size label template

Fig. 5-13

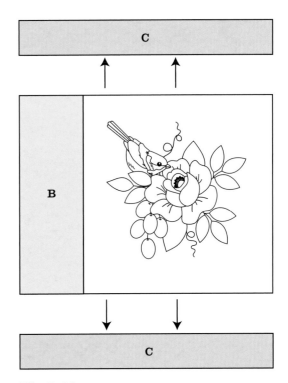

Fig. 5-14

TEA WITH MISS D, 75" x 75", made by the author

Hand Appliqué with Embroidery ◉ Sandra Leichner

TEA WITH MISS D

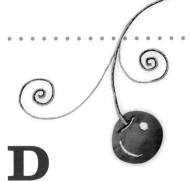

My dearest friend Miss D,

You are invited to my garden for afternoon tea. The table will be laid with lovely china, silver, and embroidered linens pressed ever so perfectly. We will enjoy, without a care for a calorie, our favorite petite pastries that taste oh, so heavenly. What fun we will have with our girly things among the roses enjoying our lovely spot of afternoon tea.

Embroidery Stitches

Stem
Straight
Whipped stem
Whipped chain
Buttonhole
Buttonhole wheel
Backstitch
French knot
Satin
Twisted chain
Lattice couching
Lazy daisy
Threaded running stitch
Beading/sequins

Fabric Requirements

The background fabric requirements for the center block area are generous because most of the construction is done using reverse appliqué; more fabric allows for ease of alignment.

Background Fabrics

Teacup center circle – ¾ yard
Strawberry shortcake scallop – ¾ yard
Accent border center section – ¾ yard

*Spoon Border – 1¼ yards

Accent border spoon section – 1¼ yards

*Cupcake Border – 3½ yards

* Border 1 – 1¾ yards
* Border 2 – 1¾ yards
* Border 3 – 2¼ yards

*cut on the lengthwise grain

Appliqué Fabrics

Assorted fat quarters and scraps

I suggest purchasing ½ yard each of your main palette colors for the appliqué. Supplement those with a variety of scraps and fat quarters of various colors, shades, and small prints. Give yourself plenty of fussy-cutting options.

(Fabric Requirements continued on page 72.)

Cupcake Border Tea Bags

Silk organza – ¼ yard

Solid white or cream fabric – fat eighth

Embellishment Requirements

Suggested Threads

Six-ply cotton embroidery floss

50- or 60-wt. sewing thread

Superior clear MonoPoly thread for beading

Suggested Needles

#10 sharps for one strand of embroidery floss
or sewing weight thread

#9 crewel (embroidery) needle for
2–3 strands of embroidery floss

#10 sharps for beading with MonoPoly
thread

Other Embellishments

Size 11 glass seed beads

Optional Fabrico™ fabric marker(s)

¾" hand crocheted lace (vintage or your own
would be lovely)

Notes:

Center spoon section = 36½" square

Spoon scallop square = 34" square

Cupcake border square = 9¼" x 56"

Center to scallop square = 22¾"

Scallop = 21¾"

Appliqué Elements

Tip: There are times when it is far easier to do the embellishment steps before stitching the appliqué piece(s) to the background. Read carefully through these instructions. The embroidery keys are numbered in stitch order to help you know which details should be stitched when.

Placement diagram. If you need a full-size placement diagram, enlarge 1034%.

Fig. 6–1

Fig. 6-2. Spot of Tea template

Center Block

Tea Bag Label (Fig. 6–1)

Step one: Trace around the Spot of Tea tea bag label template onto your fabric. Trace the tea bag label text onto your fabric with a fine (.01–.005) tip black fabric pen. Heat set the text for five–ten seconds with a dry hot iron. With a washable marker, lightly trace the embroidery lines and center circle placement onto the fabric (Fig. 6–2).

Step two: Mark the fabric for the center circle with the leaves, trim it with seam allowance, and appliqué the circle to the label in the appropriate place.

Step three: Before cutting out the label appliqué piece for placement on the background, complete the embroidery (Fig. 6–3).

Cut out the appliqué piece, including the seam allowance, and pin it in the appropriate place on the background.

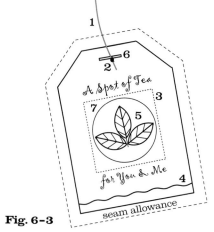

Fig. 6-3

Tea Bag Label		
embroidery key #	# strands/thread	stitch
1: tea label string	2/cotton floss	whipped chain
2: tea label string knot	3/cotton floss	French knot (3 wraps)
3: tea label outline square	1/sewing weight	stem or backstitch
4: tea label bottom	1/sewing weight	running stitch
	1/sewing weight	threading of running stitch
5: label leaf fill	2/cotton floss	satin
label leaf stem/veins	1/sewing weight	straight
6: tea label staple	2/cotton floss	whipped stem
7: center circle outline	1/sewing weight	stem or backstitch

Teacup (Figs. 6–4 and 6–5)

Teacup template on page 76.

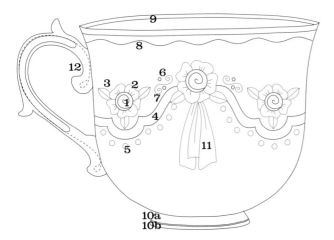

Fig. 6–4

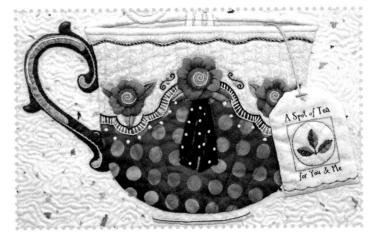

Fig. 6–5

Teacup		
embroidery key #	# strands/thread	stitch
1: rose center	1/cotton floss	whipped stem
2: rose petal veins	1/cotton floss	straight
3: rose leaf veins	1/sewing weight	straight
4: buttonhole trim	2/cotton floss	buttonhole
5: trim dots	3/cotton floss	French knot (3 wraps)
6: curly detail dots	2/cotton floss	French knot (3 wraps)
7: curly detail	1/sewing weight	whipped stem
8: wave border	2/cotton floss	whipped stem *(use a contrasting color to whip)*
9: teacup back lip	1/cotton floss	stem or backstitch
10a: teacup foot top line	1/sewing weight	stem
10b: teacup foot bottom	1/cotton floss	stem
11: ribbon	1/sewing weight	stem
12: teacup handle	2/cotton floss	stem for outline
tear shapes	2/cotton floss	satin fill

Teacup

Teacup template
Enlarge 200%

Strawberry Shortcake

Strawberry shortcake template – shown at 100%

Hand Appliqué with Embroidery ⊛ Sandra Leichner

Strawberry Shortcake

(Figs. 6–6 and 6–7)

Strawberry shortcake template on page 76.

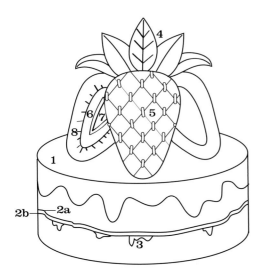

Fig. 6–6

Fig. 6–7

Strawberry Shortcakes		
embroidery key #	**# strands/thread**	**stitch**
1: cake top	2/cotton floss	twisted chain
2a: whipped cream layer	2/cotton floss	whipped stem (whipped loosely)
2b: jelly layer	2/cotton floss	2 rows of stem next to each other
3: jelly drips	2/cotton floss	satin
4: strawberry leaf veins	1/sewing weight	straight
5: center strawberry	1/cotton floss	lattice couching laid threads
	1/cotton floss	couching stitches (seeds)
6: berry halves outer "v"	2/cotton floss	whipped stem
7: berry halves inner "v"	1/cotton floss	backstitch
8: berry halves spokes	1/sewing weight	straight

Decorative Motif A (Figs. 6–8 and 6–9)

This is the decorative embroidery design between each of the strawberry shortcakes around the center circle.

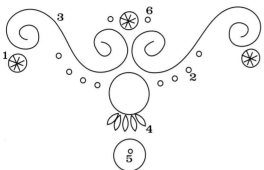

Fig. 6–8

Fig. 6–9

Decorative Motif A		
embroidery key #	**# strands/thread**	**stitch**
1: buttonhole flower centers	2/cotton floss	buttonhole wheel
	3/cotton floss	French knot (3 wraps)
2: dots by swirls	2/cotton floss	French knot (3 wraps) *(try two colors combined)*
3: swirls	2/cotton floss	whipped stem *(whip with a different color)*
4: circle petals	2/cotton floss	Lazy Daisy
5: dot on circle	3/cotton floss	French knot (3 wraps)
6: dots	3/cotton floss	French knot (3 wraps)

Decorative Motif A template
shown at 100%

Hand Appliqué with Embroidery ❈ Sandra Leichner

Spoon Border

Spoons (Figs. 6–10 and 6–11)

Fig. 6–10

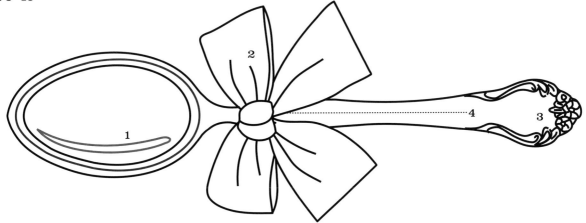

Fig. 6–11. Spoon border template – shown at 100%

Spoons Border		
embroidery key #	**# strands/thread**	**stitch**
1: spoon bowl	2/cotton floss	stem stitch to fill (approx. 2.5 rows)
2: bowl fold lines	1/sewing weight	stem
3: handle detail	1/sewing weight	backstitch
4: handle highlight	1/sewing weight	stem

Decorative Motif B (Figs. 6–12 and 6–13)

This is the decorative embroidery design around the bottom edges of the scallops.

Use a couple of different values of green for the leaves to add depth. Using different values for the flowers is also a nice touch.

Fig. 6–12

Fig. 6–13. Decorative Motif B template – shown at 100%

Decorative Motif B

embroidery key #	# strands/thread	stitch
1: dots	2/cotton floss	satin
2: leaves	2/cotton floss	lazy daisy
3: stems	2/cotton floss	stem
4: French knot flowers	2/cotton floss	French knot (3 wraps)
5: center daisy	2/cotton floss	lazy daisy
center dots	2/cotton floss	French knot (3 wraps)

Sugar Cookie (Figs. 6–14 and 6–15)

I used a combination of #11 Delica® iridescent beads and #11 satin finished beads to create the sugar on the cookie and some sparkle.

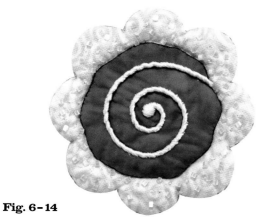

Fig. 6–14

Fig. 6–15. Sugar Cookie template – shown at 100%

Sugar Cookie

embroidery key #	# strands/thread	stitch
1: frosting swirl	3/cotton floss	whipped stem
2: cookie outline	1/sewing weight	stem or backstitch
3: sugar	2/strands of MonoPoly	beads

Cupcake Border

Chocolates (Fig. 6–16)

If you choose to lightly stuff your chocolates as I did, you will need to complete the embroidery before stitching them down to the background.

Step one: Trace around the circle template onto the chosen fabric for the chocolate (Fig. 6–17).

Step two: In a darker chocolate color embroider a swirl (Fig. 6–18).

Fig. 6–16

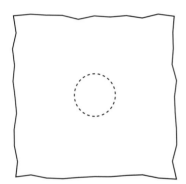

Fig. 6–17

Fig. 6–18

Chocolates – dark swirl		
embroidery key #	# strands/thread	stitch
1: dk. chocolate swirl	2/cotton floss	whipped stem

Step three: Add the secondary swirl in a white or cream color, ninety degrees over the dark chocolate swirl (Fig. 6–19).

Step four: Trim the seam allowance around the chocolate and pin it onto the background fabric (Fig. 6–20).

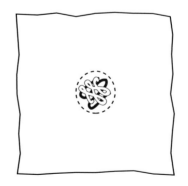

Fig. 6–19

Fig. 6–20

Chocolates – light swirl		
embroidery key #	# strands/thread	stitch
1: light top swirl	1/cotton floss	whipped stem

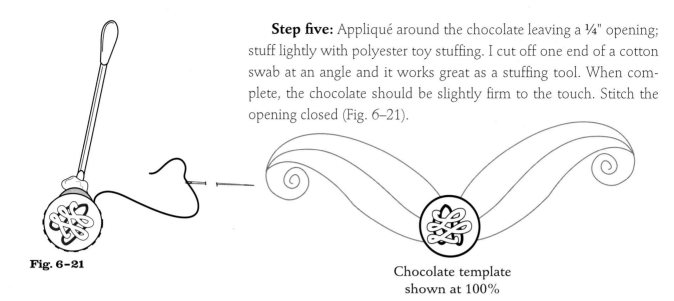

Step five: Appliqué around the chocolate leaving a ¼" opening; stuff lightly with polyester toy stuffing. I cut off one end of a cotton swab at an angle and it works great as a stuffing tool. When complete, the chocolate should be slightly firm to the touch. Stitch the opening closed (Fig. 6–21).

Fig. 6-21

Chocolate template
shown at 100%

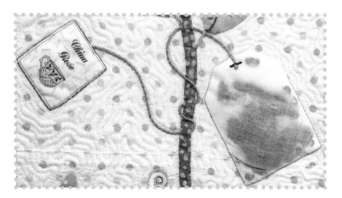

Fig. 6-22

Tea Bags (Fig. 6–22)

Step one: Iron a freezer-paper tea bag template to the back of white cotton fabric and trim it with a scant ¼" seam allowance. Do not remove the freezer-paper template (Fig. 6–23).

Step two: Layer an oversized untrimmed piece of silk organza over the white cotton side (front) of the cotton/template sandwich and baste through all layers, including the template (Fig. 6–24).

Step three: Trim the organza's seam allowance to ¼" all the way around.

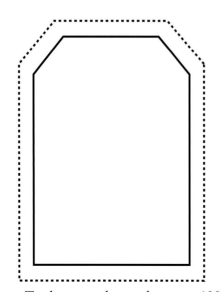

Fig. 6-23. Tea bag template – shown at 100%

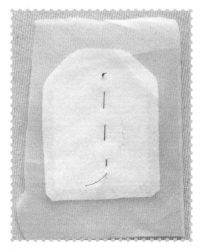

Fig. 6-24

Hand Appliqué with Embroidery ❀ Sandra Leichner

Step four: Turn the seam allowances of both the organza and cotton to the back of the freezer paper and baste to hold the tea bag shape. When this basting is complete, remove the previous basting stitches (Fig. 6–25).

Step five: Pin the tea bag in place on the background. Starting at the bottom right, just before the point, stitch all the way around the perimeter of the tea bag. Stop approximately ½" to ¾" from where you started stitching to leave an opening (Fig. 6–26).

Step six: Remove the basting stitches. Gently bring the opening's seam allowances to the front. Remove the freezer-paper template—tweezers are perfect for this job. Gently separate the organza and cotton layers and stuff lightly with small bits of yarn and/or beads to resemble loose tea leaves (Fig. 6–27). Make sure to pre-test your "tea" to make sure it is colorfast!

Why is this important? I always make my quilts to be washable. The "tea" in this quilt has been washed. Even using a wet blocking method will cause most fugitive dyes in many threads and yarns to run. I remember the first tea bag experiment (no washing), just a spill of water. It was baaaad.

Step seven: Slide the seam allowances back under to the back and stitch closed (Fig. 6–28).

Tea Bag Labels (Fig. 6–29)

For the labels of the tea bags, trace the images and text to your fabric with a fine (.01–.005) fine tip black pen (Fig. 6–30, page 84). Heat set for five-ten seconds with a dry hot iron.

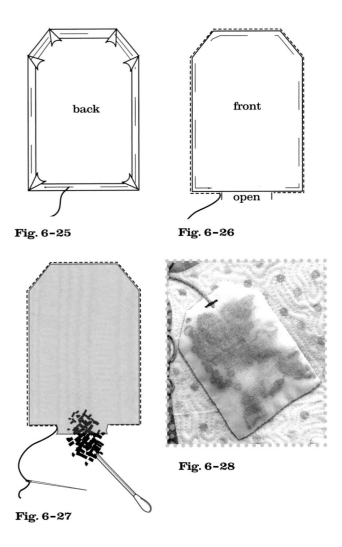

Fig. 6-25   Fig. 6-26

Fig. 6-27

Fig. 6-28

Fig. 6-29

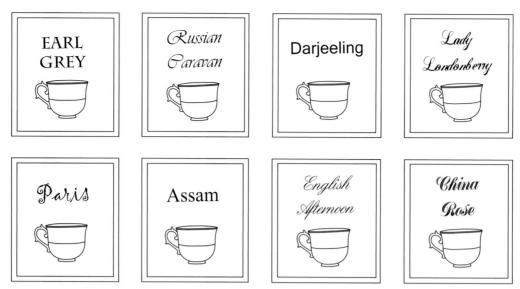

Fig. 6-30. Tea bag labels – shown at 100%

Fig. 6-31

Do not cut out your labels for stitching until you have completed the embellishing steps. I colored in the upper and lower portion of the teacup image with a Fabrico® marker to match my center teacup (Fig. 6–31).

If you use the markers to color in your labels, don't forget to heat-set the ink. Now you can add the embroidery details.

Cut out labels to include the seam allowance. Pin to the background and needleturn in place.

Tea Bag Label		
embroidery key #	# strands/thread	stitch
upper teacup		
1: rose leaves	1/sewing weight thread	lazy daisy
2: roses	1/cotton floss	French knot (2 wraps)
lower teacup		
3: lattice work	1/sewing weight	lattice couching

       Hand Appliqué with Embroidery ❈ Sandra Leichner

Cupcakes (Fig. 6–32)

Stuffing the appliqué slightly behind the frosting on the cupcakes will give them some added interest and dimension. They will look like you could take your finger and sneak some frosting! If you choose to create chocolate cupcakes, the "cake" appliqué seam allowance will not shadow through the frosting (Fig. 6–33).

Fig. 6-32

Fig. 6-33. Cupcake template – shown at 100%

Cupcakes		
embroidery key #	**# strands/thread**	**stitch**
1: rose center swirl	1/cotton floss	whipped stem
2: rose leaves	1/sewing weight	stem
3: underlining of frosting	1/sewing weight	stem
4: rose petals	1/sewing weight	straight
5: cupcake cup	2/cotton floss	stem (2 rows side by side)
shadow lines	1/sewing weight	stem

Fig. 6-34

Leaves (Figs. 6–34 and 6–35)

Notice how I used a lighter vein color on the dark leaf and a darker color on the light leaf? Switch things up and create some interesting color play with the thread and fabric.

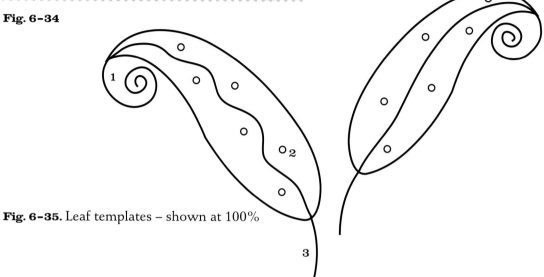

Fig. 6-35. Leaf templates – shown at 100%

Leaves		
embroidery key #	# strands/thread	stitch
1: whimsical vein	1/cotton floss	whipped stem
2: dots	3/cotton floss	French knot (3 wraps)
3: leaf stems	2/cotton floss	whipped stem

Cherries (Figs. 6–36 and 6–37)

Fig. 6-36

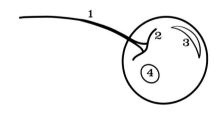

Fig. 6-37. Cherry template – shown at 100%

Hand Appliqué with Embroidery ❋ Sandra Leichner

Cherries		
embroidery key #	# strands/thread	stitch
1: stem	2/cotton floss	whipped stem*
2: cherry top highlight	1/cotton floss	stem
shadow below highlight	1/sewing weight	stem
3: "moon" highlight	1/cotton floss	stem (fill area)
4: circle highlight	2/cotton floss	satin
Create 2 rows of stem stitch where the stem meets the cherry and whip the two together as you are whipping the rest of the stem.		

Tendrils and Daisy Stems

(Figs. 6–38 and 6–39)

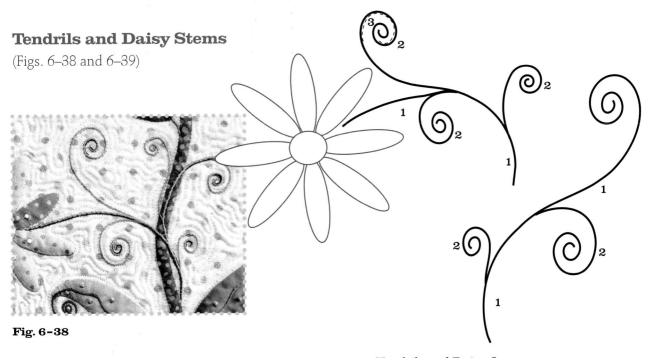

Fig. 6-38

Fig. 6-39. Tendrils and Daisy Stems

Tendrils and Daisy Stems		
embroidery key #	# strands/thread	stitch
1: larger stems/tendril	2/cotton floss	whipped stem
2: smaller stems/tendrils	1/cotton floss	whipped stem*
3: shadow detail	1/sewing weight	stem or backstitch
To create the shadowing with a darker color, stitch only a small portion of the inside of the tendril's curve as shown in #3. Do this for all or some of the tendrils to create another layer of color and depth.		

Fig. 6-40

Strings and Staples

(Figs. 6–40 and 6–41)

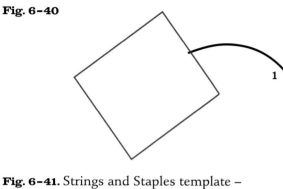

Fig. 6-41. Strings and Staples template –
shown at 100%

Strings and Staples		
embroidery key #	# strands/thread	stitch
1: tea bag string	2/cotton floss	whipped stem
2: staple	2/cotton floss	whipped stem

Daisy (Figs. 6–42 and 6–43)

Fig. 6-42

Fig. 6-43. Daisy template – shown at 100%

Hand Appliqué with Embroidery ❖ Sandra Leichner

Daisy		
embroidery key #	**# strands/thread**	**stitch**
1: swirl center	1/cotton floss	whipped stem
2: stamens	1/sewing weight	straight
3: stamen tips	2/MonoPoly	bead and sequin

Quilt Assembly

This quilt can be made into several sizes by completing the central block only, or through the spoon border, or through the entire design, or by adding additional borders. Your choice!

Center Block

Cut the background for the teacup and spoon circle center appliqué 24" x 24". Press horizontal and vertical alignment lines.

Tip: if you want a more secure and visual method of marking your centering alignment marks, baste a running stitch over the horizontal and vertical fold marks.

Proceed to appliqué the teacup and spoon to the background fabric. When the appliqué is complete, apply the embroidery embellishments (Fig. 6–44).

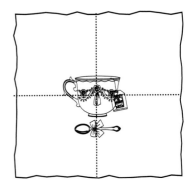

Fig. 6–44

Cut the shortcake appliqué background fabric 24" x 24". Create vertical and horizontal centering lines.

Make a freezer-paper template of the center circle and mark the centering marks on the freezer paper. Iron the template onto the strawberry shortcake background fabric, lining up the centering marks carefully. Mark around the circle template and remove the freezer-paper template (Fig. 6–45).

Layer the shortcake background fabric over the teacup center background lining up the centering lines carefully. Pin or baste securely outside of the circle area (Fig. 6–45).

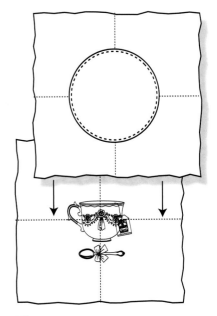

Fig. 6–45

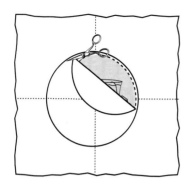

Fig. 6–46

Fig. 6–47

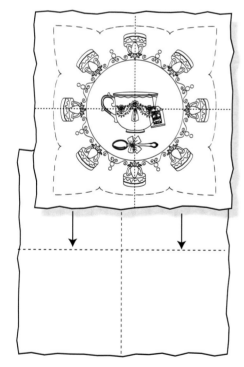

Fig. 6–48

With your fingers, take a pinch of some of the shortcake circle center background and free it from the teacup background. Snip a slit into it with the scissors. You are creating an opening within the center of the shortcake fabric in which to insert your scissors and trim away the seam allowance from the shortcake background circle. Make sure to trim your seam allowance inside the circle's marked line and not on the outside (Fig. 6–46).

Reverse appliqué the shortcake circle's seam allowance to the teacup background. When finished, turn over the work and trim away the excess teacup background ¼" from the outside of the circle's stitching line (Fig. 6–47).

Appliqué the embellished shortcakes and then apply the embroidery around them.

Mark the edge scallops onto the block. Make sure you have strong vertical and horizontal centering marks. I create a freezer-paper template to do this and it works very well for me.

Cut a square of accent fabric 24" x 24" and create centering guides. Layer the block onto the accent fabric and match the centering guides. Pin well along the scallops and center (Fig. 6–48).

Trim the seam allowance as you stitch the scallop edge to the accent fabric background.

When the scallop appliqué is complete, square the block to 23¼" x 23¼" (includes seam allowance) and put this center block aside while you work on the spoon borders.

Optional embellishment: Hand stitch your own handmade crochet lace, vintage lace, or other lace you find appealing to the scalloped edge.

Spoon Borders

All borders are constructed as butted borders for this quilt.

Cut 2 border backgrounds 7½" wide x 27" long for the right and left sides.

Cut 2 border backgrounds 7½" wide x 38" long for the bottom and top borders.

The sugar cookies will be appliquéd to the top and bottom border **background pieces only.**

Hand Appliqué with Embroidery ● Sandra Leichner

When appliqué is complete, apply the embroidery embellishments to the spoons and sugar cookies, but do not add the embroidery swags at this time.

Square up and cut the side borders to 6½" x 23½". Attach to the center block.

Square up the top and bottom borders to 6½" x 35¾". Attach to the quilt center block and sides (Fig. 6–49).

At this point there is excess yardage all the way around the quilt, so the scallops can be marked and you have hoop room for the embroidery step. With a washable marker, measure your quilt and mark a guideline for the border area of 34" x 34".

Mark the scallops to sit along this guideline.

Cut a 38" x 38" piece of accent fabric. Press horizontal and vertical centering lines. Layer the quilt top over the accent fabric centering the two fabrics together. Pin or baste well (Fig. 6–50).

Appliqué the scallop edge to the accent fabric, trimming the seam allowance as you stitch.

Trace the swag motifs to the scallops and complete the embroidery.

Appliqué circles onto the accent fabric border and square up the quilt top. It should measure 37" x 37" (Fig. 6–51).

Cupcake Borders

Cut the border fabric for the right and left cupcake borders 11" x 39".

Cut the top and bottom border fabric 11" x 60".

Appliqué each border, keeping in mind that the corner areas of the border where the seams will occur will have to be sewn after the cupcake borders are attached to the rest of the quilt. I leave the corner appliqué for after the attaching stage.

I create a separate small, easy-to-handle vinyl overlay of the corner areas to place my final appliqué pieces after the borders are attached.

Complete the embroidery and embellishments.

Square up and cut left and right borders 10¼" x 37". Attach the borders to the completed section of the quilt.

Fig. 6–49

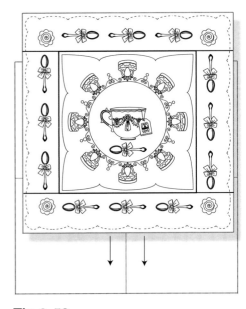

Fig. 6–50

Fig. 6–51

Fig. 6-52

Square up and cut the top and bottom borders 10¼" x 56½". Attach the borders (Fig. 6–52).

Complete the remaining appliqué on the corner areas. Apply embroidery embellishments. This completes the appliqué portion of the quilt. If you wish, you could quilt and bind the project at this stage or add additional borders (Fig. 6–53).

The steam rising from the center teacup is quilted on my example, but certainly could be appliquéd as well (Fig. 6–54).

Optional Borders

I added additional plain fabric borders to play with free-motion machine quilting and to add another layer of overall color. This is where you can add your own personal touch to the quilt.

Fig. 6-53   RIGHT: **Fig. 6-54**

Hand Appliqué with Embroidery ❀ Sandra Leichner

Gallery

UNEXPECTED BEAUTY, 51"x 67", 2006

PHARAOH, 76"x 82", 2002

AMERICAN STILL LIFE, 80" x 80", 2003

POPPY SOLILOQUY, 30" x 41", 2008

Resources

Cartwright's Sequins
http://www.ccartwright.com

DMC
http://www.dmc-usa.com

Superior Threads
http://www.superiorthreads.com

Clover Needlecraft, Inc. USA
http://www.clover-usa.com

Aurifil USA Inc.
http://www.aurifil.com/aurifilusa.htm

Morgan Hoops and Stands, Inc.
http://www.nosliphoops.com

Fabrico® Fabric Markers
Tsukineko, Inc.
http://www. tsukineko.com/

Pat Campbell's Marking Pencil
http://www.patcampbell.com

Roxanne International
http://www.thatperfectstitch.com

Cosmo Embroidery Threads
Lecien Corporation Art & Hobby Division
http://www.lecien.co.jp/en/hobby/index.htm

Colonial Needle Company
http://www.colonialneedle.com

Fire Mountain Gems & Beads
http://www.firemountaingems.com

Beyond Beadery
http://www.beyondbeadery.com

About the Author

Sandra Leichner is an internationally awarded and recognized Master Appliqué Artist. She is known for masterpiece quilts that showcase her unique, illustrative approach with hand appliqué and hand embellishment techniques.

Combining an art background with years of working with textiles and fibers, Sandra creates stunning quilts that are both artistic and traditional in style with breathtaking workmanship quality.

PHOTO: JENNA LEICHNER

Her work has consistently garnered major juried national and international awards including national Best of Show awards, as well as the RJR Best Wall Quilt at the AQS quilt show in Paducah and a Master's Award at the International Quilt Festival in Houston.

Sandra's quilts are included in The National Quilt Museum and other permanent collections. She has appeared on two PBS specials and *The American Quilter* television program, and her quilts have been published in many sources worldwide.

Sandra lives in the heart of the Willamette Valley in Oregon with her children Andrew, Jason, and Jenna, and her husband, Brett. She is assisted by three cats and a Pug named Daisy.

OPPOSITE AND RIGHT: TEA WITH MISS D, detail. Full quilt page 70.

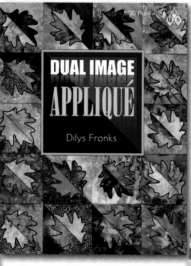